CONTENTS

GW01003436

Unit	Title	
1.1	DEVELOPMENT IS AROUND US	
1.2	DECIDING TO DEVELOP	6
1.3	DEVELOPMENTS CAN BE ISSUES	8
1.4	DEVELOPMENT IS WORLD-WIDE	10
1.5	DEVELOPMENT FILE	12
2.1	BRITAIN'S FOOD	14
2.2	FAIR SHARES?	16
2.3	GROWING MORE FOOD	18
2.4	SELF-HELP	20
2.5	THE FOOD BUSINESS	22
3.1	NORTH AND SOUTH	24
3.2	WORLD POPULATION	26
3.3	POPULATION GROWTH	28
3.4	PEOPLE MOVING	30
3.5	THE UK CASE	32
4.1	GOING PLACES	34
4.2	THE PEOPLE-EATING RAILWAY	36
4.3	ACROSS A CONTINENT	38
4.4	CHAOS IN LAGOS?	40
4.5	THE CHANNEL TUNNEL	42
5.1	USING ENERGY	44
5.2	POWER FOR BRAZIL	46
5.3	SUGAR CARS	48
5.4	ENERGY IN THE UK	50
5.5	UK CHOICES	52
6.1	WORK IS ...	54
6.2	DEVELOPMENT FOR JOBS	56
6.3	BEYOND THE FACTORY	58
6.4	A CAR FOR MALAYSIA	60
6.5	CAR WORLD	62
7.1	THIS IS PERU	64
7.2	POPULATION AND DEVELOPMENT	66
7.3	MIGRATION	68
7.4	A VALLEY IN THE ANDES	70
7.5	DEVELOPMENT IN PERU	72
8.1	COMPARING THREE COUNTRIES	74
8.2	ENERGY RESOURCES	76
8.3	ENERGY DEVELOPMENTS	78
8.4	INDUSTRIAL LOCATION: STEEL	80
8.5	CHANGING PATTERNS	82
9.1	ONE SMALL WORLD	84
9.2	TRADING WORLD	86
9.3	POPULATION DISTRIBUTION	88
9.4	AID AND DEVELOPMENT	90
9.5	REAL DEVELOPMENT AND ME	92
	Glossary	94

1.1 DEVELOPMENT IS AROUND US

Targets

* To be aware that **developments** are around us in the local environment.
* To understand that developments can affect any part of our environment and people's lives.
* To consider what development means.

Developments are around us in our local environment. Map **A** and photos **B** to **D** show 3 developments taking place in one place - Tynemouth on the coast of North East England.

A

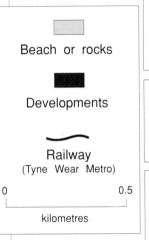

Beach or rocks

Developments

Railway
(Tyne Wear Metro)

0   0.5
kilometres

1. MARINERS POINT. New one and two bedroomed apartments for retired people have been built for sale. There are special security features and a warden service. The site used to be wasteland and a derelict building.

2. TYNEMOUTH STATION. The old Victorian railway station had been allowed to fall into decay. It is being restored to its former glory. New shops are planned for the old station offices. The station is being redeveloped.

3. The BEACONSFIELD is an area of open space on the sea front. At the moment it is grassed and used for caravans. Sometimes events like exhibitions are held there. The land could be sold by the local council so that a hotel or leisure development can take place.

Developments around Tynemouth.

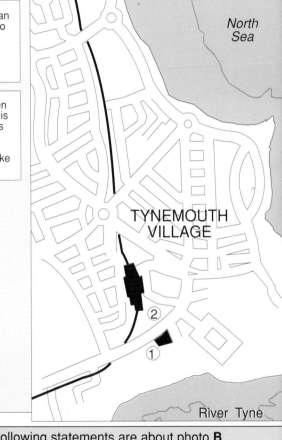

CORE ACTIVITIES

1 Look at map **A**. Each of the developments has a number.
● Complete the table below.

Location	Name	Type of development	Situation before development
1	Tynemouth railway station	Restoring the old station and developing shops	The station had decayed
2			
3			

2 Now look at the photos, **B** to **D**.
● Match each of the numbers in the table above to one of the photos.

3 The following statements are about photo **B**.
● Make a list of them.
● Next to each statement write down if it is true or false.
  - It shows land for sale.
  - A hotel is definitely going to be built there.
  - The land is now a **greenfield site**.
  - A leisure centre might be developed there.
  - This development could help tourism in Tynemouth.
  - No one is likely to object if a hotel is built here.
● Write a sentence to explain what a greenfield site is. (☞ GLOSSARY)

FOLENS GEOGRAPHY

GEOGRAPHY

DEVELOPMENT

STEVE RICKERBY

ACKNOWLEDGEMENTS

The authors and publishers would like to thank the following for permission to reproduce photographs and other material:

Action Aid (2.2C)
Aspect Picture Library (4.4B)
Cameron Hall Dent Ltd (6.3D)
Carlos Reyes/Andes Press Agency (7.1C)
Eurotunnel Information Centre (4.5A; 4.5B)
Hutchison Ltd (1.4A; 1.4B; 2.5A; 4.3D; 4.4A; 5.1A; 5.1C; 5.3C)
J. Allan Cash Ltd (5.1B; 6.1A; 6.1B; 6.1C)
Japan Information and Cultural Centre, London (8.3A; 8.4A)
Maggie Murray/Format Photographers (4.5D)
Muslim Aid, London (9.4A)
Nissan (6.2A; 6.2B)
Oxfam (7.3A; 9.4C)
Panos Pictures (5.3A)
Picturepoint (2.3A; 8.3C)
RM Communications (6.4A)
Reed Farmers Publishing Group (2.2B)
Robert Harding Picture Library (7.1C)
South American Pictures (7.1C)
Still Pictures (3.4A; 3.4D; 4.1D; 5.2C)
Susan Griggs Agency (7.1C)
Tony Stone (4.1A; 7.1C; 7.2B)
UK Atomic Energy Authority (5.5A)

Additionally thanks are due to: Debbie Rickerby
                                   Development Education Project
                                   Eurotunnel
                                   Geraldine Gibson
                                   New Internationalist
                                   North Tyneside Library
                                   Greenpeace
                                   H.J. Heinz Co.
                                   Help the Aged
                                   Oxfam
                                   The *Guardian*

Illustrators: Keith Allison and Tricia Allison of Marque Moon Design.

The publishers have made every effort to contact copyright holders but this has not always been possible.
If any have been overlooked we will be pleased to make any necessary arrangements.

© 1992 Folens Limited, on behalf of the author.
First published 1992 by Folens Limited, Dunstable and Dublin.
Folens Limited, Albert House, Apex Business Centre, Boscombe Road, Dunstable LU5 4RL, England.

ISBN 1 85276085-0

Printed in Singapore by Craft Print.

4 Look at photo **C**.
   - Make a list of all the groups which have helped pay for the **redevelopment** of the station at Tynemouth.
   - Put a tick next to all the groups which are not private companies.

5 Make a sketch of the new apartments shown in photo **D**.
   - Use it as part of your design for a newspaper advertisement which the developers can use to help sell the apartments to people aged over 55.

6 Write three sentences.
   - Each sentence has to start:
     Developments are ...
   - Each sentence has to end with one of the three possible correct endings in this list:
     ... changes.
     ... always done by the government or local councils.
     ... never going to spoil the environment.
     ... not always welcomed by everybody. around us.

EXTENSION ACTIVITIES

7 Think about the area where you live or around your school.
   - What developments are taking place?
   - Make a table like the one in Activity 1 to present information about them.
   - Make a sketch map to show where they are.

8 Use copies of a local newspaper to find out about local developments and present your findings in a table.
   - Does the newspaper say if anyone is objecting to the developments?
   - Explain any arguments about developments you find.

1.2 DECIDING TO DEVELOP

Targets

* To realise that developments happen because of decisions.
* To understand that development decisions are based on reasons which are often economic.
* To be aware of who may make development decisions.

The Beaconsfield site on the northern edge of Tynemouth could be developed as a hotel. Lisa Tanner is a **developer** who is thinking about building a hotel on the Beaconsfield site.

Lisa needs to think about whether the hotel would make a profit. This depends on keeping **costs** down and attracting a lot of people to stay there. Table **C** is a profile which Lisa uses to help her decide. It lists the **factors** she thinks about in deciding whether or not to develop a hotel on the Beaconsfield site.

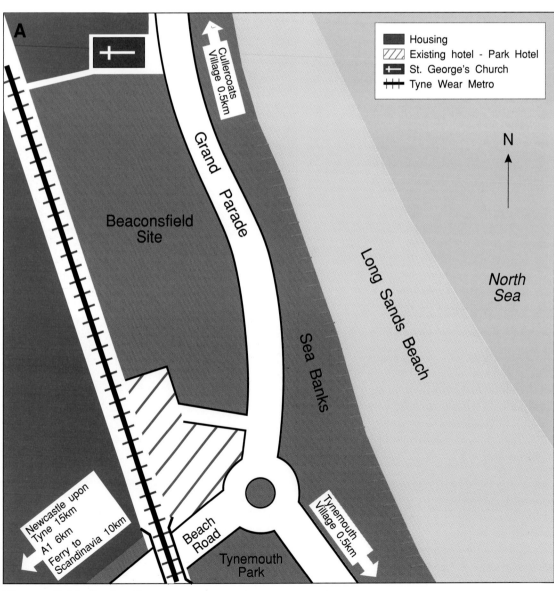

Beaconsfield site: location

CORE ACTIVITIES

1 Look at map **A**.
- Copy and complete this:
  The _____ site lies just to the _____ of _____. The site is next to a road called _____ _____ , just around the corner from _____ ____ which is the way towards the city of _____ ____ ____ .
  Choose your answers from these:

Tynemouth	east	Grand Parade
south	Newcastle upon Tyne	
west	Beach Road	
north	Beaconsfield	

2 Read **B**.
- Imagine the interview was on TV. Draw the two people on the screen standing at the Beaconsfield site.
  (*HINT*: Look back to **B** in Unit 1.1.)
- Show what they are saying.
- Now answer these questions about **B**:
  - Which two groups of people would Lisa Tanner expect to stay there?
  - Why might holidaymakers like to stay there?

3 Look carefully at table **C** and at map **A**.
- On a copy of table **C**, complete the empty boxes.
  (*HINTS*: Think of the Comment column as a way of explaining your ticks and crosses.)

4 Study your table carefully.
- If you were Lisa Tanner, what would you think of the Beaconsfield site? Decide between:
  Ideal
  Good, but not perfect
  Not good enough
- Now explain your decision.
- For each of the factors in your table, write a sentence to say how the Beaconsfield site would help, or not help, a hotel to make a profit.

5 Who will decide if a hotel is built on the Beaconsfield site?
- Will it be:
  - the local council?
  - developers like Lisa Tanner?
  - local people who live in Tynemouth?
- How do you feel about that? Are they the people who should make such decisions? Why?

Lisa Tanner being interviewed on local radio

C	Factor	Present at Beaconsfield	Comment
	Large, flat site	✓	Development would be easy to start
	Sea views		The Long Sands beach can be seen
	Good communications		
	Quiet situation		Metro railway runs along the back of the site
	Close to a labour force		Tynemouth and Cullercoats villages
	Near a city for business customers		
	Local council agreement	✓	

Lisa's hotel site profile

6 For a development you know about, imagine yourself as the developer.
- Make a table like the one in **C** to show how the site measures up to the factors you had to think about.

7 Extend your sketch from Activity 2.
- Make it into a series of pictures showing how you think the full interview between Lisa Tanner and Richard the reporter might have gone.

1.3 DEVELOPMENTS CAN BE ISSUES

Targets

* To realise that people may have different views about developments.
* To be aware that developments may have costs as well as benefits.
* To balance these costs and benefits to form your own view about a development issue.
* To understand the feelings of people affected by development decisions.

People can have different views about developments. The idea that a hotel could be developed on the Beaconsfield site is an issue. Some people feel it would be a good idea; others are not so sure.

Lorraine works in the Park Hotel. This is next door to the Beaconsfield site, as map **A** in Unit 1.2 shows. She has mixed feelings about the hotel development idea.

People's views about the Beaconsfield development

CORE ACTIVITIES

1 Read **A**.
* Write two sentences to say what Lorraine thinks about the hotel development. In the first sentence say what she thinks is good about it. In the second sentence say what worries her about it.

2 Look back to map **A** in Unit 1.2.
* Draw your own sketch map to show where the Park Hotel is in relation to the Beaconsfield site.

3 The people in **A** have raised a number of issues about the hotel.
* On a copy of table **D** fill in the empty boxes using what they have to say.

4 Look at the **scales diagram** in **C**.
* Draw more diagrams to show the balance of views of each of these people in **A**:
  - Lisa
  - Mehmet
  - Andreas
  - Richard

Park Hotel

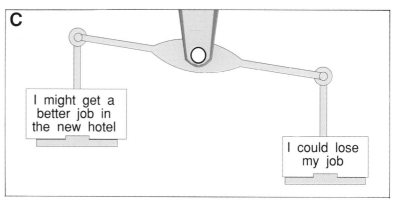

Lorraine weighs things up

D Issue	Costs	Benefits
Jobs	A new hotel would mean more competition. Jobs in other hotels could be lost.	A new hotel could bring new jobs.
Our environment		
Profits		
Who decides?		

Costs and benefits table

5 Imagine a conversation between Andreas and Lorraine about the hotel development idea.
   ● What would they each say? How would each try to convince the other that she/he was right?
   ● Either write a script for this conversation, or draw it like a comic strip.

6 Look back to your copy of table **D**.
   ● For each issue, think of the balance between the costs and the benefits. Draw your own scales diagrams to show your decisions.
   ● How does it all add up? Do you think that the balance is in favour of the idea, or do you think it is against it?

EXTENSION ACTIVITIES

7 For a development you know about, make your own costs and benefits table.
   ● For each of the issues draw a scales diagram.
   ● Write a report saying what you think about this development and why, using your table and diagrams as illustrations.

8 A magazine editor has heard Richard's radio programme about the Beaconsfield hotel development. She wants to publish an article about it, putting forward both sides. To do this she has asked Lisa Tanner to write one half of the article and Lorraine to write the other. They have both been told they can use pictures, maps and diagrams.
   ● Choose to be either Lisa or Lorraine and write your half of the article.
     (*HINT*: Remember you are now putting forward only one side. Your job is to put the case as well as possible so that readers will agree with you.)

Targets

* To realise that developments may be found all over the world.
* To understand that developments are very varied.
* To be aware of issues raised by developments.

An African development

Developments may be found around us in our local environment. They can also be found around the world. **A** and **B** show two developments in Africa. One is a large-scale development and the other is a small-scale development.

The two developments in **A** and **B** are very different in size and cost. However, they are both developing the same **resource**.

Map **C** gives information about a number of developments around the world (including **A** and **B**), and about issues they raise.

An African development

CORE ACTIVITIES

1 Look at photos **A** and **B**.
  ● Copy each of the following descriptions and say which is of **A** and which is of **B**:
    - Photo ___ is a large-scale development, costing a great deal of money.
    - Photo ___ is a small-scale development, costing a small amount of money.

2 Here are some jumbled resource names:
  Inrisame gyener atrwe birmte
  ● Make a list of the unjumbled resource names and tick the name which matches both **A** and **B**.

3 Think about **A** and **B**.
  ● Which is the development that ordinary, local people are likely to have most control over?
  ● Draw a sketch of this development and write a caption to explain your choice.
  ● Who do you think controls the other development?

4 Look at map **C**.
  ● Write two sentences about the costs and benefits of the developments shown in **A** and **B**.

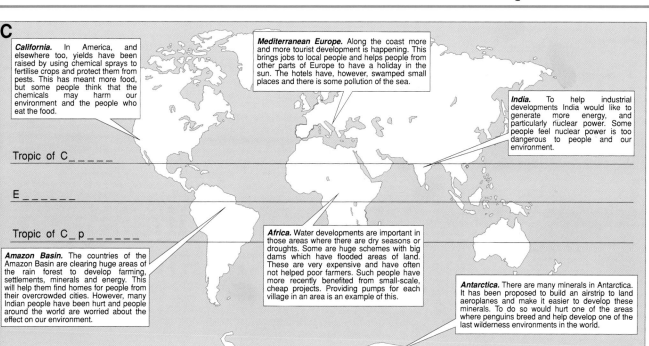

C

California. In America, and elsewhere too, yields have been raised by using chemical sprays to fertilise crops and protect them from pests. This has meant more food, but some people think that the chemicals may harm our environment and the people who eat the food.

Mediterranean Europe. Along the coast more and more tourist development is happening. This brings jobs to local people and helps people from other parts of Europe to have a holiday in the sun. The hotels have, however, swamped small places and there is some pollution of the sea.

India. To help industrial developments India would like to generate more energy, and particularly nuclear power. Some people feel nuclear power is too dangerous to people and our environment.

Tropic of C_ _ _ _ _

E _ _ _ _ _ _

Tropic of C_ p _ _ _ _ _ _

Amazon Basin. The countries of the Amazon Basin are clearing huge areas of the rain forest to develop farming, settlements, minerals and energy. This will help them find homes for people from their overcrowded cities. However, many Indian people have been hurt and people around the world are worried about the effect on our environment.

Africa. Water developments are important in those areas where there are dry seasons or droughts. Some are huge schemes with big dams which have flooded areas of land. These are very expensive and have often not helped poor farmers. Such people have more recently benefited from small-scale, cheap projects. Providing pumps for each village in an area is an example of this.

Antarctica. There are many minerals in Antarctica. It has been proposed to build an airstrip to land aeroplanes and make it easier to develop these minerals. To do so would hurt one of the areas where penguins breed and help develop one of the last wilderness environments in the world.

Some developments around the world

D

D	A	E	Q	U	A	T	O	R	W	W	T
F	S	B	U	M	C	I	T	C	R	A	N
A	A	C	I	R	E	M	A	N	O	P	R
R	M	N	E	N	O	G	I	C	P	A	O
R	E	O	T	E	A	P	G	P	A	I	C
E	R	U	A	A	O	I	E	S	C	L	I
C	I	U	S	A	R	I	D	F	I	A	R
N	C	I	S	A	N	C	I	N	F	R	P
A	A	T	R	A	I	C	T	A	I	T	A
C	R	A	T	L	A	N	T	I	C	S	C
T	A	C	I	P	L	R	H	A	C	U	M
O	P	C	I	T	C	R	A	T	N	A	E

Wordsearch

5 You will need a copy of map **C**.
- On it label the world's continents and oceans.
- Complete the names of the special lines of **latitude** shown. (*HINT*: All the names you need are hidden in **D**.)

6 Read **C** again.
- Make a table to show a cost and a benefit for each of the developments shown.

EXTENSION ACTIVITY

7 Research some developments of your own.
- Find out where they are, and an important cost and benefit of each.
- Plot your developments on a world map. (*HINT*: Places to look include other geography books and newspapers.)

1.5 DEVELOPMENT FILE

Targets

* To be able to profile a development.
* To be aware of the key questions to ask about a development.
* To understand why learning about developments is part of geography.

A shows information about a development as presented in a newspaper.

B is a development profile. It can be used to record information about developments.

C says what developments are and asks why learning about developments is part of geography.

A

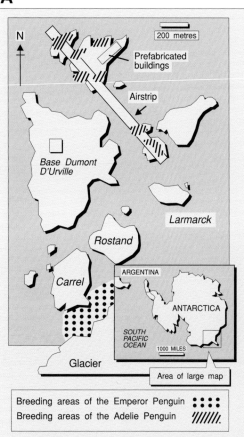

Penguins that face death on the rocks

Paul Brown reports from Antarctica on French plans to start blasting for a new airstrip later this month that threaten many of the birds breeding on the site

THE French government is blowing up six islands off the coast of Antarctica. They are doing this to build an airstrip. Blowing up the islands flattens them for the airstrip and the debris can be used to fill in the sea between the islands so the runway can be built across all six.

The islands are the breeding grounds for birds and penguins have been killed by the explosions.

The French say the airstrip is needed to help develop valuable oil and mineral resources in Antarctica and to help scientists to come and study this remote part of the world.

The environmental group Greenpeace disagree. They say the development is too harmful to birds, the number of penguins has already more than halved during construction. Also, they say the French started the development before they had properly thought about the effect it would have on the environment. Greenpeace are concerned that if the French development goes ahead, other countries like the USA and the UK will also want to build these airstrips in Antarctica.

A development

CORE ACTIVITIES

1 Look at **A** carefully.
 ● Use it to complete each of these sentences:
   The development is in _____ .
   An _____ is being built.
   This is being done by the _____ government.
   They want to develop oil and _____ resources.

2 An **environmental group** is said to be opposed to the development.
 ● Which is it?
 ● Make a list of three things the group does not like about the development.

3 On a copy of the development profile **B**, fill in the empty boxes by collecting information from **A**. (*HINT*: Your answers to Activities 1 and 2 should also help.)

4 What is your view about the development in **A**?
 ● Draw a scales diagram to show how you think the costs and benefits balance. (*HINT*: Look back to Unit 1.3.)

B Location

Development change

From: *A wilderness. Bird breeding ground. Small scientific station.*
To:

Decision makers

People affected *No-one living there, but environmentalists and scientists worried. Mining companies could make money and provide jobs.*

Are they the decision makers? *No, but mining companies are influential.*

Benefits

Costs

A development profile

C

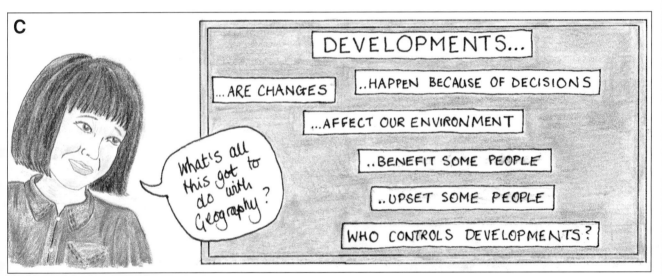

Claire and the wall display

EXTENSION ACTIVITIES

5 Read the wall display in **C**.
● Write five sentences to explain what developments are.
● What is your answer to Claire's question? (*HINT*: These words could be used in your answer, think of them as clues:

people	change
places	effect

*our **environment**.*)

6 Use more copies of the development profile to collect information about other developments.
(*HINT*: Use Units 1.1 to 1.4 of this book, newspapers or developments you know about yourself.)

7 Design a poster called Developments and Geography.
● Your poster should show people how developments can be part of geography.

2.1 BRITAIN'S FOOD

Targets

* To realise that Britain **imports** food.
* To use an atlas to locate countries around the world.
* To be aware that there are people in Britain who do not eat well.

What have you eaten today? It may well have been produced somewhere else in the world. **A** shows some fruit that you might find on a supermarket shelf. Map **B** shows the location of these countries.

C shows what one person in Britain, Mark, ate in one day.

Fruit from around the world

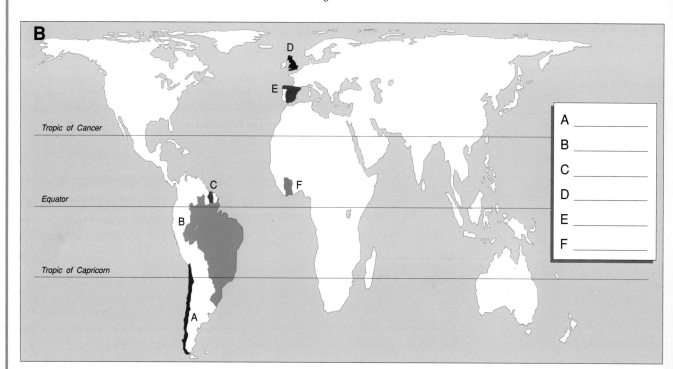

CORE ACTIVITIES

1 Look at **A**.
  ● Use it to complete this table:

Fruit	Country of origin

2 In your atlas find a good map showing the countries of the world.
  ● Use it to complete the key to the country names on map **B**.

3 Some fruit is grown in Britain.
- Write down three fruits that you know are grown in Britain.
- Think about this:
  There has been a cold, wet summer and Britain's fruit harvests are poor.
  - How will Britain get its fruit?
  - What will happen to the price?
  - Will this affect everyone equally?
  - Who will it affect most?
  - It is not the government which will arrange to supply people with the fruit. Who is it?

4 Look at **C**.
- Do you think Mark has eaten well?
- Write down three foods he has eaten that you think are very healthy to eat.
- Now write down three foods that you think are less healthy.
- Mark says it does not matter that he eats foods which some people think are unhealthy, so long as he does not eat too much of them. What do you think? Explain your view.

5 ☞ GLOSSARY
- Find out what **self-sufficient** means.
- Explain if Britain is self-sufficient in food.

C

Name	Mark da Costa.
Day	Tuesday May 16th
Breakfast	Didn't bother.
Mid-morning	Packet of crisps. Chocolate biscuit. Coffee.
Lunch	Bacon butty. Can of pop. Fruit pie.
Afternoon	Packet of sweets. Cup of tea.
Evening	Chicken and pasta. Some salad. Banana. Milk. Biscuits.

Mark's food

EXTENSION ACTIVITIES

6 Make a chart like **C** to show the food you ate yesterday.
- Do Activity 4 again, this time for yourself.

7 Investigate which other countries the food eaten in Britain comes from.
- Make a list of foods and their countries of origin.
(*HINT*: You could do this activity at home or in a shop or supermarket. If you do it in a shop, ask someone in charge if you can first.)

8 Consider these statements:
If Britain cannot feed its own people by growing its own food, its population must be too high and should be cut.
Britain can only feed its people because it is rich enough to buy food from other countries. Not every country is so lucky.
- What do you think about these statements? Are they true? Why do you think that? Do other people agree with you?

2.2 FAIR SHARES?

Targets

* To understand that the world has sufficient food, but it is not shared out equally.
* To realise that it is poor people who go hungry.
* To be concerned about the sharing out of the world's food and for the welfare of the hungry.

Map **A** shows the average **calorie** intake from food in the countries of the world. That means it shows how much energy the average person in each country gains from food. It can be seen that some countries have a higher average calorie intake than others. There is **inequality** between countries in food.

The **EC** countries, including the UK, grow too much grain. Some of it is stored away.

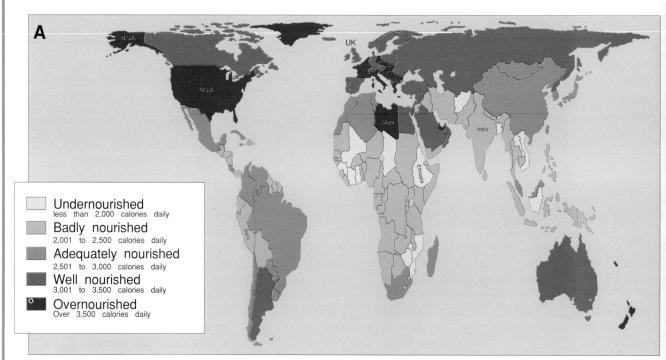

Undernourished
less than 2,000 calories daily

Badly nourished
2,001 to 2,500 calories daily

Adequately nourished
2,501 to 3,000 calories daily

Well nourished
3,001 to 3,500 calories daily

Overnourished
Over 3,500 calories daily

World calorie consumption

EC grain mountain

CORE ACTIVITIES

1 Look at the key to map **A**.
  ● How many calories a day are needed for a person to be well nourished? Choose from:
    less than 2 000
    2 001 to 2 500
    2 501 to 3 000
    3 001 to 3 500
    over 3 500

2 Complete the following table to show how well nourished each of these countries is:

Country	How well nourished
USA India Ethiopia United Kingdom Libya Peru	

3 Find one country shown by map **A** as badly nourished.
  Use an atlas to help you name it.
  ● How many calories does the average person take in daily?
  ● Does this mean every single person there is badly nourished?
  ● Who is badly nourished?

4 ● On a blank world map showing country boundaries, shade all the countries which are shown as badly or undernourished the same colour.
  ● Use a second colour to shade those shown as adequately, well or overnourished.
  ● Look at your map and think about this hypothesis:
    Most of the world's underfed countries are in the southern part of the world.
  ● Do you agree, partly agree, or disagree?
  ● Explain your reasons.

5 Read **C**.
  ● What does the advert say about:
    - the problem of undernourishment in Ethiopia?
    - how people reading the advert can help?
    - what is good about sponsoring as a way to help people?

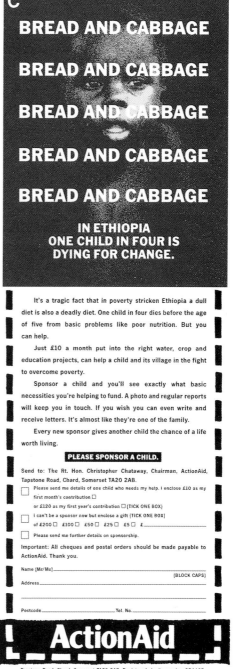

Newspaper advertisement
What is it designed to do?

EXTENSION ACTIVITY

6 Look at photo **B**. Think about map **A** and advert **C**.
  ● Write a letter to your MEP (Member of the European Parliament) to say how you feel about EC countries producing and storing grain. You might ask why it happens and if it is going to continue in the future.

2.3 GROWING MORE FOOD

Targets

* To understand that growing more food has not helped to feed everyone properly.
* To realise that farmers in countries which are undernourished work very hard.

Many of the world's countries are undernourished or badly nourished. Well-off people eat well in these countries; poor people often do not. Perhaps if they grew more food they would eat better, or would they?

Photo **A** shows rice farmers hard at work planting rice in a paddy - a flooded field for growing rice. The work it takes to grow the rice is shown by **B**.

The flood plain of the River Ganges in India is a good place to grow rice. Each year the river floods the land on either side depositing fertile silt.

D shows that India was growing a lot more rice in the 1980s than in the 1960s. This was because of something known as the **Green Revolution**.

Rice planting in the Madras area of India

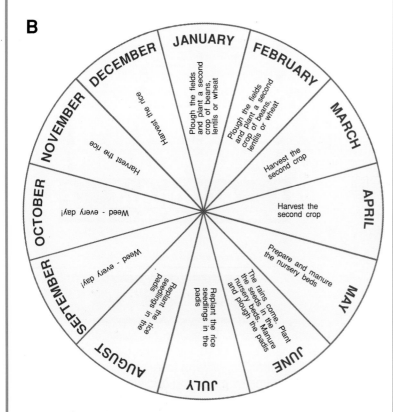

B

The rice farmer's year

CORE ACTIVITIES

1 Look at photo **A**.
 ● Copy each of the statements below.
 ● Next to each statement say if you think it is true or false.
  - These farmers are picking rice.
  - Land on the flood plain is very flat.
  - Farm work is always done by men.
  - Working like this all day must be hard.
  - This farming is highly mechanised.

2 What month is it now?
 ● Use **B** to write down what work you would be doing if you were one of the farmers in photo **A**.

3 Use the climate data in **C** to plot a **climate graph** for the Cherrapunji which is on the Ganges Plain.
 (*HINT*: ☞ GLOSSARY.)

4 Cherrapunji has a Monsoon climate.
 ● Use the data in **C** and your climate graph to complete this description of the Monsoon climate of Cherrapunji:
 Temperatures are between ___ °C in January and ___ °C in August. The heaviest rains (over 1 000mm per month) are in the months from ___ to _____ .

5 Find a good map of India in your atlas.
 ● Use it to help you complete the place
    names and the key on a copy of the map
    in **C**.

6 Look back to map **A** in Unit 2.2.
 ● Write down the average calorie
    consumption in India. Choose between:
    - less than 2 000 calories a day
    - 2 000 to 2 500 calories a day
    - 2 500 to 3 000 calories a day
 ● How well nourished are people in India? Is
    the average person:
    - badly nourished?
    - adequately nourished?
    - well nourished?

7 Look at the bar graph in **D**.
 ● Use it to complete this data table:

Period	Rice area (million hectares)
1960s 1970s 1980s	0.9

 ● How much more land was given to growing
    rice in the 1980s than the 1960s? Was it:
    - twice as much?
    - ten times as much?
    - twenty times as much?

C

P – – – –
B – – – –
D
N
Ch
A
INDIA
C
B – – – –
B
H
M
Bay of Bengal
Ba
Indian Ocean
S – –
L – – – –

0   400   800 1200 1600 km

● **Towns and Cities**
D _____
C _____
B _____
M _____
H _____
A _____
Ba _____
Cherrapunji

CLIMATE DATA: Cherrapunji		
MONTH	**TEMPERATURE (°C)**	**RAINFALL (mm)**
January	12	18
February	13	54
March	17	185
April	18	666
May	19	1 280
June	20	2 695
July	20	2 446
August	21	1 781
September	21	1 100
October	19	493
November	16	69
December	13	13

Cherrapunji, on The Ganges Plain: location and climate

EXTENSION ACTIVITIES

8 Compare **B** and your climate graph.
  ● Make a list of links between changes in the
     climate and the work the farmers do.
9 Find out more information about the monsoon
   climate.
  ● Try to discover:
     - which parts of the world have such a
       climate
     - what makes the monsoon rains come
       (*HINT*: Use your atlas and other books.)

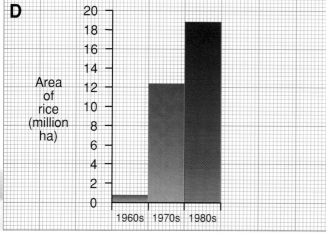

D

Area of rice (million ha)

20
18
16
14
12
10
8
6
4
2
0

1960s 1970s 1980s

Growing more rice

2.4 SELF-HELP

Targets

* To understand why many poor farmers have not benefited from the Green Revolution.
* To be aware of alternatives to the Green Revolution which may help poor farmers more.

Countries like India have increased food production because of the Green Revolution. Some people, poor people, still go hungry. In fact some poor farmers actually lost their land because of the technical advances made by the Green Revolution.

A shows how two Indian farmers were affected by the Green Revolution.

If the Green Revolution has not helped poor farmers, what can be done?

The development profile (**C**) can be used to compare different developments in feeding ourselves.

A

" THE GREEN REVOLUTION HAS HAD GOOD EFFECTS FOR ME - I'VE BEEN ABLE TO GROW MORE RICE - ABOUT 3 TIMES AS MUCH. I'VE BEEN ABLE TO BUY FERTILISER AND A TRACTOR. THIS HAS BEEN BECAUSE I OWNED ENOUGH LAND TO BE ABLE TO AFFORD THE NEW SEEDS AND BECAUSE I HAD MORE RICE TO SELL AFTERWARDS. YES, I'M MUCH BETTER OFF."

" I'VE LOST MY LAND. I'M HAVING TO MOVE AWAY TO THE CITY. THE GREEN REVOLUTION HAS MADE ME WORSE OFF THAN EVER. WHEN THIS 'MIRACLE' RICE CAME OUT I COULDN'T AFFORD TO BUY THE SEED. PEOPLE WHO COULD MADE MONEY TO BUY FERTILISERS AND MACHINES SO THEY GREW MORE AND MORE. THE PRICE FELL FOR THE LITTLE I HAD TO SELL. I HAD TO BORROW MONEY, BUT I COULDN'T PAY IT BACK."

A tale of two farmers

CORE ACTIVITIES

1 Read **A**.
* Write a sentence to say which farmer was well off and which was poor.
* Use what the two farmers say in **A** to complete this table:

	Well-off farmer	Poor farmer
Effects of the Green Revolution		Lost land. Moved to the city. Worse off than ever.
Reasons		
Did the Green Revolution help?		

Village meeting

2 Place yourself in the role of the poor farmer. Your well-off neighbour has done well out of the Green Revolution and cannot understand why you are leaving the area.
● Explain why you have to go, why the Green Revolution has not worked for you. Describe your feelings - you have lived on the land all your life and were all right until outsiders came up with the ideas of the Green Revolution.

3 Using **B**:
● Write about two ways for feeding the village that the farmers at the meeting suggest.

4 You have attended the meeting. Afterwards a friend who was not there asks you this question:
How can a group of poor farmers hope to do better than the scientists and experts who brought us the Green Revolution?
● Tell your friend the reasons that were presented at the meeting.

5 On a copy of **C**:
● Fill in the empty boxes. Some have already been done as examples.
● On another copy of **C**, enter facts about one of the self-help schemes suggested in **B**.

6 With the help of this unit and the Glossary
● Write sentences to explain what these words mean:
   - **Green Revolution**
   - **self-help**
   - **land reform**
   - **irrigation**
   - **appropriate technology**.

C	
Location	India, Ganges Plain.
Development change	Green Revolution.
From:	Low Rice Yields.
To:	High Rice Yields.
Decision makers	The Indian Government. Rich farmers.
People affected	Rich and poor farmers.
Are they the decision makers?	Only the rich farmers.
Benefits	
Costs	

A development profile

EXTENSION ACTIVITIES

7 A television reporter visits a village in India to make a programme about the Green Revolution and self-help alternatives. She interviews two farmers, one well-off and one poor.
● What questions should she ask?
● Write down the answers the farmers might give.
● The programme has to say what the Green Revolution is, how it has helped some farmers and why it has not helped others, as well as what self-help alternatives there are and why self-help can be a good idea.

8 People in the UK and the rest of the EC want to help poor farmers like those in **A** and **B**.
● Design a poster to explain to them why their money may be better spent on small self-help schemes than on research into new sorts of miracle rice.

2.5 THE FOOD BUSINESS

Targets

* To realise that food production can be a big business.
* To understand that food supply is becoming more controlled by a small number of big food businesses.
* To be concerned about the effect of this on poor people.

In Europe and North America in particular, farming (or **agriculture**) has become big business. A lot of money (or **capital**) has been spent on **mechanisation**, **fertilisers** and **pesticides**.

The food which is produced is often processed and sold by big food companies. **B** shows some **processed foods**. The whole big business of producing and selling food is called **agribusiness**. Names of some big companies in agribusiness are also shown in **B**.

Big companies like those in **B** often own farms and plantations in a number of different countries, so they are **multinational companies**. The effect of multinational food companies on poor people causes concern (**C**), but advertisement **D** shows that not everyone thinks multinationals are a bad thing for development.

Farming is big business

CORE ACTIVITIES

1 Make a sketch of photo **A**.
* Write a caption for your sketch to explain how it shows that farming has become big business.

2 ☞ GLOSSARY
* Match up each of these words to the correct meaning:

    Mechanisation ...   **Capital ...**
    Agribusiness ...   **Fertiliser ...**
    Pesticide ...

    - means a chemical to help crops grow better.
    - means big companies producing and selling food.
    - means using more machines.
    - means a chemical to protect crops from attack.
    - means money to spend on trying to make a business grow.

    EXAMPLE: Mechanisation means using more machines.

3 Use **B** to help you complete this table:

Processed food	Multinational company
Coffee	Nestlé

* Write a sentence to say what a processed food is. (*HINT*: ☞ GLOSSARY.)

4 Read what the people say in **C**.
* Do they make agribusiness seem like a good development in feeding ourselves?
* Why? List five reasons.

5 Now look at **D**.
* Why does Robert Mugabe welcome this particular multinational to his country?

B

Processed foods

Multinationals and poor people

6 Think of what you ate yesterday.
- Make a table to show which foods were processed and which were fresh.
- Also try to show the names of the food companies making the processed foods.
  (*HINT*: Look in the small print for the name of the big food company. This may be different from the first name you see.)

7 Think about this:
A multinational company decides to open a plantation in a country. The government of the country says it must meet some conditions.
- As the government, what conditions would you try to impose on the company? List them. (*HINT*: Look at **C**.)
- What good things might the company bring to your country?
- How would you feel if the multinational decided to go somewhere else, where it did not have to meet your conditions?
- Who do you think has most power - your government or the multinational?
- How do you feel about this? Do you think it is right? Why?

D # Portrait of a Partnership

"We regard H. J. Heinz Company as an important partner and an example for other foreign investors. We are very happy that Heinz has come to Zimbabwe with a development-orientated approach. That contributes to the improvement of the standard of life of the broad masses of people of our country."

HON. ROBERT G. MUGABE
Prime Minister
Republic of Zimbabwe

"Our experience in Zimbabwe has been an excellent one. We are partners with the Government in Olivine Industries Ltd, an oils, margarine and soap manufacturing company. We have been very pleased with our investment and with the constructive and helpful way the Government has assisted the company."

DR. ANTHONY J.F. O'REILLY
President and Chief Executive Officer
H.J. Heinz Company

Since this partnership began, Olivine's productive capacity has been doubled since 1982 with investment of more than 10 Million Zimbabwean dollars, exports have increased tenfold, and continuous programs of staff training have been intensified at all levels

Newspaper advertisement

3.1 NORTH AND SOUTH

Targets

* To be aware that our world's riches are unequally shared between the countries of the North and the countries of the **South**.
* To use and make **pie charts**.
* To use an atlas to name countries of the North and countries of the South.
* To be concerned at the unfair shares the North and South have.

The resources of our world are not shared equally between the different countries. Some countries are richer than others and have more resources.

The graphs in **A** are pie charts. They show how one part of the world, the North, has a greater share of our world's wealth than another, the **South**. Map **B** shows where the dividing line between the South and the North is drawn.

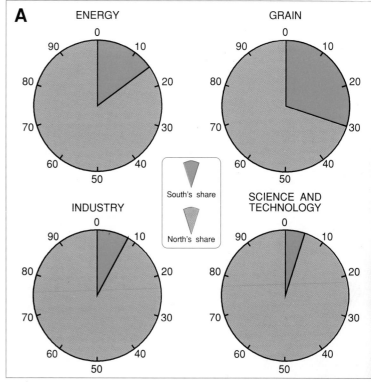

Unfair shares

In our daily lives we use resources. We use a variety of different types of resources throughout each day. **C** shows Ruth's use of resources during one hour of her day. Some of the resources Ruth uses are renewable, they can be replaced. Wood is renewable because more trees can be grown, though it may take a long time. Coal is non-renewable because people cannot make more coal, there is only so much of it.

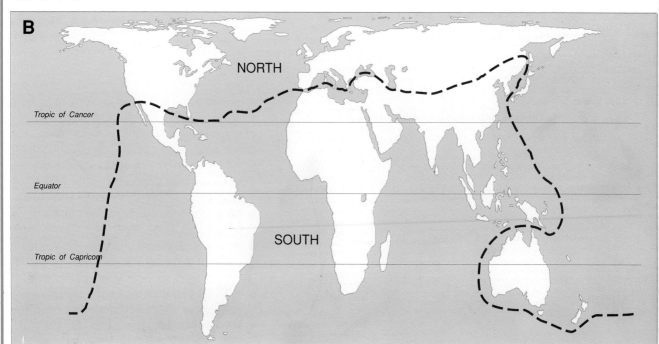

North and South

	CLOTHES	NATURAL GAS (ENERGY)	FOOD	METAL, RUBBER ETC. IN BIKE
RESOURCE				
RENEWABLE ?	WOOL OR COTTON – YES MANMADE – NO	NO	YES	METAL – NO RUBBER – YES

Ruth's hour

CORE ACTIVITIES

1 ☞ GLOSSARY.
- Write a sentence to say what resources are.
- Find ten resources in the wordsearch (**D**).

2 Use the pie charts in **A** to help you complete this table.

	South's share (%)	North's share (%)
Energy	15	85
Grain for food		
Industry		
Science and technology		
Money made from exports	18	82
Money spent on health	6	94
Money spent on education	11	89
GNP (money made from people's work)	17	83

3 Seventy-five per cent of the world's **population** live in the South.
- Write eight sentences to say how far short these people are of their fair shares.
  EXAMPLE: The South's population should be able to use 75 per cent of the world's energy, they use only 15 per cent, 60 per cent short.

4 Using an atlas and map **B**:
- Put the following countries into two lists, one headed North and the other South.
United Kingdom, Brazil, USA, India, Australia, Ivory Coast, Zimbabwe, China, USSR, Mexico.

5 Look at **C**:
- Complete this table to show the renewable and non-renewable resources used by Ruth in her hour:

Renewable	Non-renewable

D

E	T	P	E	O	S	E	R	D	Y	C
R	L	N	I	H	S	I	F	E	S	T
A	D	E	I	C	R	L	O	H	W	Y
R	T	A	C	O	L	C	O	A	A	I
L	E	C	N	T	T	E	D	P	T	G
D	Y	N	A	R	R	U	B	B	E	R
P	U	C	S	T	S	I	S	W	R	I
C	G	E	L	A	O	C	C	I	L	C
E	A	A	S	N	M	I	M	I	A	O
O	S	Y	A	R	E	B	M	I	T	Y
R	H	D	L	T	E	E	C	L	M	Y

Wordsearch

6 Choose an hour from one of your days.
- Record the resources you use, and whether they are renewable or not.

7 The graphs in **A** do not mean that every person in the North is rich and every person in the South is poor.
- Think about this and explain why not. Try to use examples of people to back up your points.

Targets

* To discover that the population of the world has grown more rapidly in recent years than in the past.
* To realise that population is growing faster in some countries than in others.
* To learn the factors which affect population growth.
* To think about choosing how to present data.
* To understand why people in the South often have more children than people in the North.

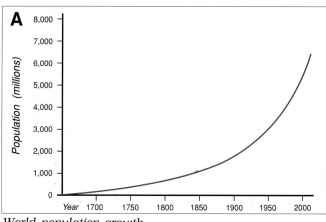

A

World population growth

Graph **A** shows how the population of the world has grown. However, population growth is not even throughout the world. It is more rapid in some countries of the world than in others.

The factors which affect population growth are shown by **C**. One of these factors is **birth rate**. This is higher in the South, where poor people often have more children because they need them, as the people in **D** explain.

B Country	Population 1988 (millions)	Population 2000 (est.) (millions)	Growth rate (%)
Australia	16.5	18.2	1.4
Brazil	144.4	178.4	2.2
China	1 083.9	1 274.4	1.2
India	814.0	995.8	2.1
Indonesia	174.8	212.4	2.1
Nigeria	110.0	163.5	3.4
Pakistan	105.7	146.2	3.1
UK	57.0	56.9	-0.2
USA	245.9	262.5	1.0
USSR	285.7	307.7	0.9

Population growth in some countries

CORE ACTIVITIES

1 Look at **A**.
● Copy the following statements about **A**.
● Next to each statement write if it is true or false.
 - The world's population has always been growing.
 - The rate of growth has lessened since 1950.
 - The population of the world today is about 5 000 million.
 - In 1900 the population of the world was already over 2 000 million.
 - The population reached 1 000 million in about 1750.
● Complete this table about the pattern of world population growth:

Population (millions)	Year
1 000	1850
2 000	
3 000	
4 000	
5 000	

C

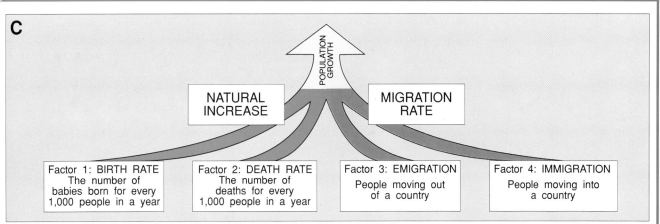

Four factors for population growth

D

Poor people need children

2 Look at **A** again.
- What is the population of the world likely to be in the year 2000?
- When will the population of the world reach 6 000 million?

3 Study the data in table **B**.
- Make a list of the ways you know of illustrating the data. (*HINT*: Think about maps, graphs and diagrams.)
- Choose one of your ideas to present the data in **B**, and explain why you chose it.
- Think about this hypothesis:
  The rate of population growth in the continents of the South has been greater than in the North.
- Do you think the hypothesis is true? Why?

4 Using diagram **C**:
- Write a few sentences explaining how four factors can decide how fast a country's population grows.

5 Read the views in **D**.
- Make a list of reasons why people in the South often need large families.

EXTENSION ACTIVITIES

6 Think about what the woman and the man say in **D**.
- How is what they say different?
- Who seems to be able to decide about how they develop their family?
- What do you think about this. Is it fair? Why?

7 Now think about yourself and people you know.
- Why do people you know want or not want children?
- Do you think the women and men have different views?
- Who do you think decides?
- Would you like children yourself? How many? When? Why?
- Who would decide? You, your partner or both of you?

3.3 POPULATION GROWTH

Targets

* To realise that, as people become better off, population growth slows down.
* To test **hypotheses** about developments which may make population growth slow down.
* To be aware of the role of women in slowing population growth.

Poor people in the South World often have more children than people who are better off. They have these children for good reasons (Unit 3.2).

As people become better off, the rate of population growth generally slows down.

Table **B** shows how the birth rates and population growth rates of four South World countries all slowed down over a period of 20 years. Also shown are two factors which might help explain why two of the countries changed more than the others.

A and **B** together show some of the developments that can help people choose to have fewer children.

Population growth slows down when lots of people decide to have fewer children because they are better off. Who decides? Whose choice is it? The women in **C** explain their choices.

Developments in slowing population growth

B Country	Birth rate (births per 1 000 people)		Population growth rate (%)		Did the poorest become much better off?	Was there much land reform
	Year 1	Year 20	Year 1	Year 20		
Taiwan	40	23	3.3	1.8	Yes, three times as much	Yes
Mexico	44	32	3.4	2.5	Hardly at all	No
Brazil	40	32	2.9	2.4	Hardly at all	Yes
South Korea	41	19	2.8	1.4	Yes, twice as much	No

Data from the world

CORE ACTIVITIES

1 Look at **A**.
* Match each of the sketches with one of these developments:
  - When food and health are better, more children live.
  - When education is developed, more people get jobs that pay more.
  - When poor farmers can use appropriate technology, they need fewer helpers on the land.
  - When women get equal chances at school and in jobs, they can have choices other than just having children.
  - When people are helped with family planning services, they can have fewer children if they want to.
  - When people can have pensions and sick pay, they need fewer children.

YES, I WANT MORE CHILDREN

WHY? BECAUSE WE ARE POOR, SO: SOME WILL DIE, I MUST HAVE MANY TO MAKE SURE ENOUGH LIVE.

I DON'T WANT ANY MORE CHILDREN

WHY NOT? BECAUSE WE ARE LESS POOR NOW, SO: NOT MANY WILL DIE MY HUSBAND AGREES, SO;

I DON'T WANT ANY MORE CHILDREN EITHER

BUT MY HUSBAND WON'T AGREE BECAUSE:

Fewer children - who decides?

2 Think about how each of the factors in **A** helps people to have fewer children.
  ● Decide which are the most important. Number each one from 1 to 6 to show how important you think it is.
  ● Write some sentences to explain the choices you have made.

3 Use **B** to help complete this new table:

Country	Birth rate fall	Population growth rate slow down
Taiwan	17	1.5
Mexico		
Brazil		
South Korea		

  ● Use the data in your table to plot two bar graphs.

4 Think about each of these hypotheses:
  When poor people are better off they have fewer children.
  Land reform has nothing to do with slowing down population growth.
  ● For each hypothesis, say if you think it is true or not. Explain the decisions you make.

5 Look at **C** and at this list of factors:
  ● On a copy of **C**, write each factor in its correct box.
  (*HINT*: Some examples have already been done.)
  - some will die, I must have many to make sure enough live.
  - not many will die.
  - we can use birth control now.
  - they can help us on the farm.
  - he does not understand all the work in looking after children.
  - we do not need as much help on the farm.
  - when we are old or sick they can look after us.
  - he wants to have more sons, like the other men.
  - we will be all right when we are old or fall ill.

6 Answer these questions about the women in **C**:
  ● How many of the women in **C** can choose on their own if they want more children?
  ● Why can the other women not choose? (*HINT*: Look for two different reasons.)
  ● What do you think? Should the women have more power in deciding how many children to have? How could women gain more power in these decisions?

EXTENSION ACTIVITIES

7 Look back to **B** and to your answers to Activities 3 and 4.
  ● With the help of your atlas, mark the countries in **B** on a blank outline map of the world.
  ● Are these countries in the North or in the South World? Which continents are these countries in?
  ● Do you think the four countries are good samples of the whole world? Why?
  ● Where could other samples have been taken to give a fuller picture?
  ● Explain how your conclusions in Activity 4 are limited, and how they could be made better.

8 Place yourself in the role of one of the women in **C**. Imagine trying to convince your husband that you should have fewer children now that you are better off.
  ● Write down the conversation you imagine would take place. (*HINT*: You could do this as a script or like a comic.)

3.4 PEOPLE MOVING

Targets

* To realise that lack of resources in some rural areas can lead people to **migrate** to urban areas.
* To be aware of **push and pull** reasons for **rural-urban migration**.
* To empathise with the experiences of rural-urban **migrants**.

The road into Abidjan

Photo **A** shows part of the city of Abidjan, the capital city of the Ivory Coast. It shows a main road leading into the city.

People have moved from rural parts of Burkina Faso to Abidjan for many years. Both Burkina Faso and the Ivory Coast used to be French colonies. Abidjan was a coastal port with a lot of trade with France, so people moved there to find jobs. They still do, more than ever, as **C** shows.

There are two sets of reasons why people **migrate** from rural to urban areas. These are **push and pull** factors. Push and pull factors that have led people like Animata (photo **D**) to migrate from Burkina Faso to Abidjan, include harsh physical conditions like drought, poverty, population pressure and the hope of better housing and a higher quality of life.

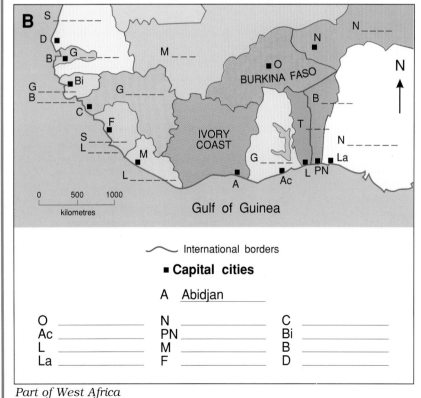

B

BURKINA FASO

IVORY COAST

Gulf of Guinea

0   500   1000
kilometres

— International borders

■ **Capital cities**

A   Abidjan

O _____	N _____	C _____
Ac _____	PN _____	Bi _____
L _____	M _____	B _____
La _____	F _____	D _____

Part of West Africa

CORE ACTIVITIES

1 Look at photo **A** and at the following list of words.
 ● Use the words to make a description in sentences of photo **A**.

main road	bustling
mini-buses	very busy
low buildings	taxis
noisy	transport
buying and selling	congested
coaches	roadside

 (*HINT*: Try to use all the words. You can put them in any order that makes sense to you.)

2 In your atlas, find a good map of West Africa's countries - a **political map.**
 ● Use it to complete the country names on map **B** and to finish the key showing capital cities.

C

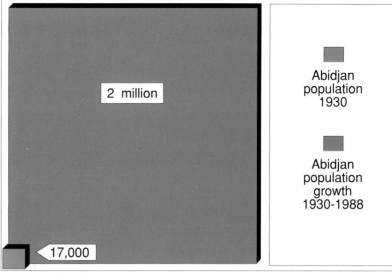

■	Abidjan population 1930
■	Abidjan population growth 1930-1988

2 million

17,000

The growth of Abidjan

3 Complete this table about why people migrate:

Push Factors	Pull Factors
	Jobs

4 Look at **C**.
- What was the population of Abidjan in 1930?
- When did the population reach 2 million?
- The population of Abidjan is going up by 80 000 people a year. When will the population reach 3 million? (*HINT*: Draw a line graph.)
- Some of the increase is **natural increase** from babies born in the city, but most is not. Why is Abidjan growing so much?

5 Read about Animata (**D**).
- Place yourself in her position. A magazine reporter comes to see you. She asks you these questions:
  - Why did you come to Abidjan, Animata?
  - Can you describe your house for our readers?
  - What work do you and your husband do?
  - Do you make enough to live on?
- What answers would you give? (*HINT*: Remember Animata has food to pay for, and stock to buy for her stall.)

Animata's story

Animata moved to Abidjan, with her husband Amadou, from Burkina Faso.

Their house has one room about 2.5 metres square. The walls are made of rough wood planks. The roof leaks. Animata has four children.

Outside there is a small courtyard they share with six other homes. There is no sanitation.

Animata sells cigarettes from a small stall by the roadside. Amadou did have a good job driving a bulldozer, but he lost it when he broke his arm. Now he mends watches for people.

They earn less than £60.00 a month. Their rent is £10.00. They pay a neighbour £12.00 a month to share a tap. Electricity costs £6.00 per month.

EXTENSION ACTIVITY

6 As a villager in Burkina Faso, life is very hard for you. You are very poor. You have heard that life in Abidjan is much better, there are jobs and money can be made.
- Having made the trip, you tell a neighbour about your feelings when you arrived in Abidjan, the big city. (*HINT*: Use photos **A** and **D** to help. Think about your feelings as you leave home, on the way, when you first enter the city and after a few days there.)

Targets

* To realise that in the UK population growth has slowed down.
* To be aware of the pattern of, and some of the reasons for, continued **migration** within the UK.
* To make graphs to show population trends.
* To think about how the UK case compares with the South World.

Table **A** gives population data for Britain. Every 10 years the population is counted in a **census**. Census years are the ones shown in **A**.

Maps **B** and **C** both show the UK. Map **B** shows what the **quality of life** is like in different areas of the UK. This has been worked out using data about unemployment, housing and **infant mortality**. Map **C** shows population changes in the UK between 1981 and 1986.

A YEAR	POPULATION (Millions)
1951	44.0
1961	46.2
1971	48.8
1981	49.2

Population growth in Britain

CORE ACTIVITIES

1 Use the data in table **A** to complete this table:
  ● Choose your answers from these:
    3.4 million
    2.6 million
    1.6 million
    0.8 million
    0.4 million

Years	Population growth
	2.2 million

  ● Make two graphs:
    - a line graph using the data in table **A**
    - a bar graph using the data in the table from Activity 1.
  ● For each of your graphs, write a sentence to say what it shows about the growth of the UK's population after 1951.

2 Look at map **B**.
  ● For each of these statements, decide if you agree, partly agree or disagree:
    - The quality of life in the south east of England is better than in Scotland.
    - The best quality of life is in central London.
    - The north of England has a generally low quality of life.
    - Wales has a higher quality of life than Northern Ireland.
  ● Copy each statement. Write your choice next to it.

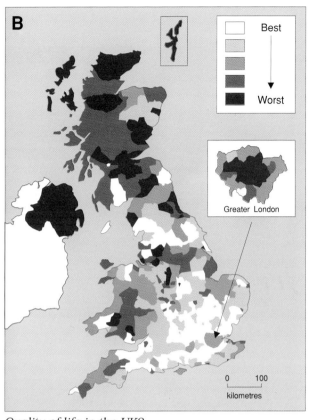

Quality of life in the UK?

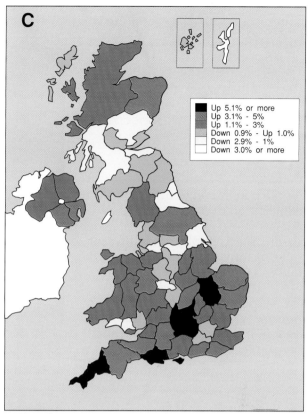

Population movement in the UK 1981-1986

3 Look at map **B**.
- Do you agree, partly agree or disagree with these statements?
  - People moved mainly from the north to the south of the UK.
  - London attracted many migrants from other areas of the UK.
  - Places where there are large urban areas lost people between 1981 and 1986. (*HINT*: Use an atlas map here.)
  - The pattern of rural-urban migration seen in West Africa repeats itself in the UK.
- Explain your decision about the last statement.

4 - On a blank copy of map **B**, showing just the regional and county boundaries, colour each area one of four colours to show:
  - areas where the quality of life is high and the population went up between 1981 and 1986
  - areas where the quality of life is low and the population went down between 1981 and 1986
  - areas where the quality of life is high and the population went down between 1981 and 1986
  - areas where the quality of life is low and the population went up between 1981 and 1986
- Think about this hypothesis:
  People move from places where the quality of life is low to places where it is high.
- Do you think your map shows this hypothesis to be true, partly true or untrue? Explain your answer.

EXTENSION ACTIVITIES

5 Look at map **B**.
- Write down the types of data that might have been used to make it.
- Think about them. For each one write a sentence to say why you think it might have been chosen.
- Are there other factors that you think should have been thought of? What are they? (*HINT*: Think about people getting on with each other and about our environment.)

6 People in the UK have been moving out of cities to countryside areas.
- Make a list of push and pull reasons for this. (*HINT*: Think about city problems and good points of country life.)
- Can anyone who lives in the city move to the country if they want to? Why not?

Targets

* To realise that people use different types of transport for going places.
* To understand that efficient transport systems allow people easy access to places they need to reach.

People may travel to different places using different sorts of transport.

Joanna, for example, uses different types of transport depending upon the type of journey she is making.

The M25 motorway circles London. Motorways are a popular transport system, but the M25 suffers from the problem of **congestion**.

Traffic in Jaipur, India

Joanna goes places

CORE ACTIVITIES

1 Look at photo **A**.
● Make a list of ways of going places. Include other ways you can think of as well as those shown in the photo, to make as long a list as you can.

2 Using the words in your list:
● Design a word puzzle for someone else to solve.
(*HINT*: It could be a wordsearch, but it does not have to be.)

3 Complete this table about the transport used by Joanna:

Type of transport	Reason for use	How often?
Bus	To go to school To go shopping Going skating	Twice a day Once a week Occasionally

4 Look at **C**.
- Use the scale on the map to find the length of the M25.
- Find a good map of south-east England in your atlas. Use it to complete the key.
- The M25 does not link places, it goes round London. Why do you think this is?

5 Look at **D**.
- Write a sentence to explain what congestion is.
- Why do you think congestion happens?
- What times of the day and week can congestion be worst? (*HINT*: Think about people's work and leisure patterns.)
- Some people think the M25 should be made wider. Suggest one reason why this might be a good idea and one reason why it might not be.
- What do you think should be done about the M25 congestion? Why? (*HINT*: Three possibilities are: nothing, build another road around London, encourage people to use the train instead of their cars.)

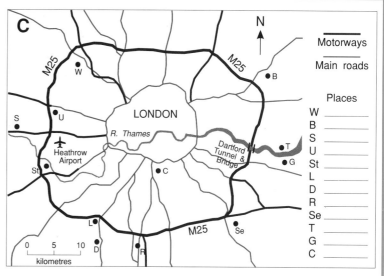

The M25

Congestion on the M25

EXTENSION ACTIVITIES

6 Think about your own use of transport as Joanna has done (**B**).
- Make your own table to show why you use different ways of going places and how often.
- Draw a pie chart to show how your journeys are shared between different transport types.

7 Here are two statements about the M25:
- The M25 is a great success - just look how many people want to use it!
- The M25 is a complete failure - it is impossible to use it to go anywhere!
- What do you think about each of these statements? Explain why.
- Write a statement of your own about the success of the M25 as a way of going places.

Targets

* To realise that **transport networks** in South World countries often developed in colonial times, for the benefit of the **colonists**.
* To understand that transport developments can bring other developments, like industry.
* To use an atlas to make a transport map of East Africa.

Map **A** shows the railways of East Africa in 1914. Kenya, Uganda and Tanzania were not separate, independent countries then. Instead they were **colonies**, part of the British Empire.

The British colonists built the railways to help them transport goods from their East African colonies to coastal ports. The goods could be taken in ships to be sold.

It was decided that a new railway would be built into Uganda from Kenya. It linked Nakuru to Kampala and Kasese. While the railway was being built the workers lived in camps along the route. Several were attacked and eaten by lions.

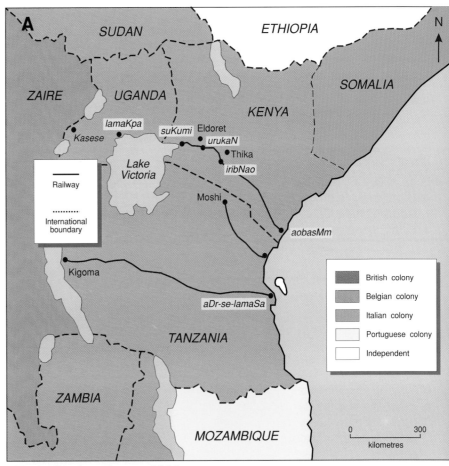

East Africa's railways, 1914

CORE ACTIVITIES

1 Look at map **A**.
* Write down the names of the countries which were British colonies.
* For each of the other countries, either write down the name of the European country which had colonised them or write down that they were independent.

2 Some town names on map **A** have been jumbled.
* Find a good atlas map of East Africa and use it to unjumble them. EXAMPLE: urukaN = Nakuru
* Write them properly on a copy of map **A**.
* Draw the approximate route of the People-Eating Railway on your copy of map **A**.

3 Answer these questions:
* What was the job of the railways in the British colonies?
* Who decided to build them?
* For whose benefit were these railways built? Explain how the railways helped these people.

4 Look at **B**.
* With the help of the data table, complete the pie chart.
* How has the railway affected the development of industry in Kenya?
* Which two towns have the biggest share of industrial jobs in Kenya?
* Write down the special **functions** these two towns have.

B

Town	Share of industrial jobs (%)	Colour on pie chart
Nairobi	57	■ (black)
Mombasa	17	■ (grey)
Nakuru	5	■ (dark)
Kisumu	3	
Eldoret	4	
Thika	9	
All others	5	
Total for Kenya	100	

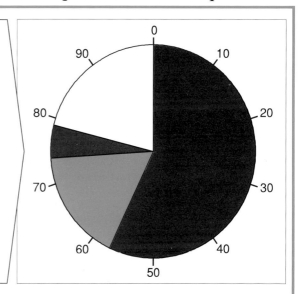

Industrial jobs in Kenya

C

Stage 1	Stage 2	Stage 3	Stage 4
Inland development leads to the first link inland	As urban developments continue, a fuller network comes into being	A few coastal ports with no real inland links	As developments inland increase, a network begins to form

A model of transport network development

EXTENSION ACTIVITIES

5 From your atlas, trace the present-day railway network of East Africa.
- Describe how it has changed from that in map **A.**
- Do you think that it still mainly links to the coastal ports, or has it developed beyond that stage? Explain your answer.

6 You will need an outline map of East Africa (Kenya, Uganda and Tanzania).
- Use an atlas to label:
  - the railway routes
  - main roads
  - main seaports and sea routes
  - main international airports

7 Study **C** carefully. The captions are in the wrong boxes.
- Draw the diagrams again, with the captions in the correct boxes.
- Write a sentence to say what a model is used for in geography.
- Which stage would you say the railway network of East Africa had developed to in 1914?
- Which stage would you say it is at now?

4.3 ACROSS A CONTINENT

Targets

* To be aware of the importance of transport links to **landlocked** countries.
* To use an atlas to learn the names of the countries and capital cities of Africa.
* To appreciate the great distances involved in crossing a continent such as Africa.

Map **A** shows the route of a proposed Trans-Africa Highway. Much of the route is already a road, but the middle sections are often dirt roads and there are gaps, the road is not continuous from coast to coast.

Traffic already uses parts of the existing route but the number of vehicles varies from location to location.

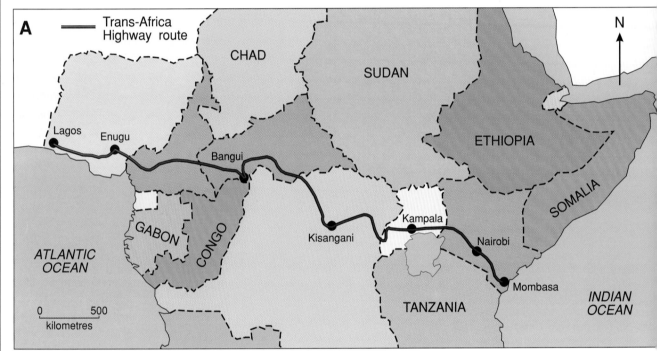

The route of a Trans-Africa Highway

B Location	Vehicles per day
Just outside Lagos	10 000
Just outside Mombasa	6 000
In Central African Republic	1

Traffic per day

CORE ACTIVITIES

1 Find a political map of Africa in your atlas.
   - Use it to name the different countries through which the road passes.

2 Some of the countries on map **A** are **landlocked**.
   - ☞ GLOSSARY. Write a sentence to explain what a landlocked country is.
   - Make a list of three landlocked countries on map **A**.
   - How can it be a disadvantage to a country to be landlocked?(*HINT*: Think about trade.)

C

	Lagos	Enugu	Bangui	Kisangani	Kampala	Nairobi	Mombasa
Lagos	- - - -	450	1,750				
Enugu							
Bangui							
Kisangani							
Kampala							
Nairobi							
Mombasa							

kilometres

Distances on the Trans-Africa Highway

Encourage trade between East Africa and West Africa.

If the road was built it would cross international borders - customs problems would have to be solved.

The highway would be very expensive to build.

Any one country could hold up traffic on the whole route if governments disagreed. The Central African Republic would rely very heavily on the goodwill of its neighbours.

Help trade to isolated regions like the Central African Republic and northern Zaire.

D

3 You will need a copy of table **C**.
- With the help of the scale on map **A**, complete the spaces in the table.
  (*HINT*: Check the examples first.)

4 Look at table **B**.
- Use the data to plot a bar graph.
  (*HINT*: Think of the answers to these questions first:
  - What problem do you have in showing the traffic of the Central African Republic?
  - How are you going to solve this?)

5 Study **D**.
- Make two lists to show the costs and benefits of the Trans-Africa Highway.

6 How would a Trans-Africa Highway help develop the Central African Republic's trade in the cotton and groundnut crops grown there?

EXTENSION ACTIVITIES

7 The Central African Republic already has a river and railway route to Pointe Noire, a sea port on the coast of Congo. The route is the Ubangi River as far as Brazzaville and then rail to Pointe Noire.
- Make a sketch map to show this route. Include the river, the railway, Pointe Noire and the countries along the way from the Central African Republic.
- Explain why the Trans-Africa Highway to Lagos could be better than the route you have drawn.
  (*HINT*: Think of the speed of water transport; the cost of unloading cargo from a boat to reload it on to a train; the importance to the Central African Republic of its trade with the EC.)

8 Make a table to show all the countries of Africa and their capital cities.
- Use a third column to show which countries are landlocked.

4.4 CHAOS IN LAGOS?

Targets

* To realise that the development of cities may lead to traffic congestion.
* To be aware of the costs of traffic congestion and of some possible solutions.

Lagos is the capital city of Nigeria. The city stands at the western end of the proposed route of the Trans-Africa Highway (Unit 4.3).

The urban area of Lagos has become congested as the city has grown. **D** shows some attempts to ease congestion which have been tried in Lagos and the effects they have had.

A

Lagos from the air

B

Congestion in Lagos. The costs of congestion are expensive new roads (expressways), accidents, pollution and lost time and money for business.

CORE ACTIVITIES

1 Look at **A** and **C** very carefully.
  ● List three different types of transport in the photo.
  ● On an outline sketch of photo **A**, add these labels:
    - expressway (motorway)
    - **Central Business District (CBD)**
    - railyard
    - shipping
    - poor housing
    - industry

2 Look at photo **B** and read its caption.
  ● ☞ GLOSSARY. Write a sentence to explain what congestion means.
  ● Make a list of the costs of traffic congestion to Lagos.

3 Look at map **C**.
  ● What are the names of the three main islands on which parts of Lagos are built?
  ● On which island are the original town, the CBD and most of the markets?
  ● How is Lagos Island linked to the mainland?
  ● Why would many commuters travel daily to Lagos Island from mainland housing areas like Maryland?

4 Look at table **D**.
- As a newspaper reporter you write an article about the traffic problem in Lagos. With the help of photo **B** and table **D** explain what it is like to be in a Lagos traffic jam and why the expensive solutions that have been tried have not worked. (*HINT*: The climate of Lagos is hot and humid.)

5 The most recent solution to have been suggested is to build an overhead railway, costing at least £250 million.
- Think about the costs and benefits of this idea, and present them in a table or as a scales diagram (Unit 1.3). (*HINT*: Look at the costs of the present congestion and think about the environment.)

D	DEVELOPMENT	RESULT
	The only road bridge to Lagos Island was widened and two new bridges built	The growth in traffic more than kept up - all three bridges are blocked every day
	A network of modern expressways (motorways) was built	Roads leading on to the expressways became jammed
	Only cars whose registration numbers began with even numbers could go on to Lagos Island on even-number dates, odd numbers on odd-number dates	People who could afford it bought two cars

Attempts to ease traffic congestion in Lagos

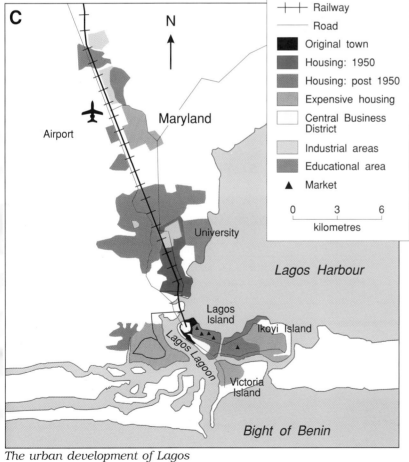

The urban development of Lagos

Legend:
- ┼┼┼ Railway
- Road
- Original town
- Housing: 1950
- Housing: post 1950
- Expensive housing
- Central Business District
- Industrial areas
- Educational area
- ▲ Market

0 3 6 kilometres

EXTENSION ACTIVITIES

6 What other methods of solving traffic congestion do you know?
- Think about a town or city you know and write down the things that have been done to relieve congestion.
- Are there any others you can think of?

7 Imagine you are living in Lagos.
- Write a letter to the newspaper where the article from Activity 4 appeared. Put forward your suggestions for solving the traffic congestion problem.

Targets

* To realise that the Channel Tunnel is a major transport development for the UK.
* To profile the costs and benefits of a major transport development.
* To understand the effects of the Channel Tunnel development on our environment and on people's lives.

1993 - the opening of the Channel Tunnel. The Channel Tunnel is a major transport development. Trains may run beneath the floor of the English Channel, linking the UK with France.

C shows how the Channel Tunnel development links together parts of the EC on either side of the English Channel. But the Channel Tunnel development has both costs and benefits, as **D** and **E** show.

A

The Channel tunnel is bored, mainly in the chalk layer of rock between Folkestone and Calais.
It comprises two running tunnels and a service tunnel.
It carries the following types of traffic:-
● Cars and coaches in passenger shuttles.
● Lorries in freight shuttles.
● Through passenger and freight trains.

The shuttles will operate between Folkestone and Calais, and terminals at these locations will provide customs immigration, shops, Duty Free and other facilities, and be connected directly to the motorway systems of the UK and France.
Shuttles will operate on a no-booking, on-demand service, leaving every 12-15 minutes at peak periods.

Through passenger trains will be operated hourly throughout the day between London and Paris. In addition, there will be through passenger services between other cities in the UK and cities in the rest of Europe.

Freight trains for wagons and containers will run from starting points around Britain directly to and from destinations on the continent.

The Channel Tunnel

Boarding the passenger shuttle

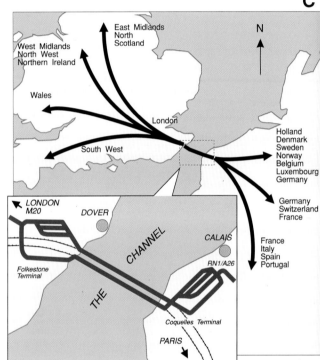

C

The Channel Tunnel links

CORE ACTIVITIES

1 Look at **A**. Read the information given there.
  ● Copy and complete:
    The Channel Tunnel stretches between _____ in the UK and _____ in France. There is not just one tunnel , but _____ . The tunnel carries cars and _____ in passenger _____ and lorries in separate trains called _____ shuttles. There are through trains too.

2 Look at photo **B**.
  ● Explain how cars travel through the Channel Tunnel.
  ● How often do passenger shuttles run? (*HINT*: Look back to **A**.)
  ● Do people have to book in advance? Why do you think that is?

3 Look carefully at **C**.
- Put these names into the order they should be for a journey from London to France by car:
  - Calais
  - RN1/A26
  - Folkestone Terminal
  - M20
  - Coquelles Terminal
- Now write a description of a car journey through the Channel Tunnel. (*HINT*: Use the sources on this page to help you.)
- Which of the countries shown are members of the EC? (HINT: ☞ GLOSSARY.)

4 Look at **D** and read its caption.
- Explain what the photograph shows.
- Imagine yourself as one of the people on this march. A TV reporter stops you to ask why you are there. Write down your reply - make sure she understands why you object to the Channel Tunnel development.

5 Read the views given in **E**.
- Use what the people say to make a list of costs and benefits. (*HINT*: Use a development profile (Unit 1.5) to record your answer to this activity and more facts about the Channel Tunnel development.)

D

Bexley says No!

E

Views about the Channel Tunnel

EXTENSION ACTIVITY

6 The TV reporter from Activity 5 is called Shona MacLeod. She presents a TV debate where all the people mentioned in **E** and some of the people from South Darenth are invited into the studio. During the show Shona tries to find out their views. She does this by asking for a comment in favour of the development and then asking one of the other people to say why she/he disagrees with that particular point. Then she moves on to the next point until everyone's view has been covered.
- How would the show go? Write down what Shona and each of the people would say. You could start with Shona introducing the programme.

5.1 USING ENERGY

Targets

* To understand that **energy** is vital to people and to development.
* To realise that the South World uses a smaller share of world energy than North World countries like the UK.
* To make and use a **scattergraph**.
* To use an atlas to find place names in South America.

A dam on the Amazon River

Energy is power. The power which drives machines, heats our homes and cooks our food - electricity, firewood, gas, **water power**, **solar power** and others are all forms of energy. Photos **A** to **C** show just three forms of energy in one South American country - Brazil.

Some types of energy are **renewable**. **Wind power** is one, because the wind will always come back. Other types of energy are **non-renewable**. Oil is one, because there is only so much oil in the **earth's crust** and people cannot put it back when it is all used.

Table **F** gives data about some South American countries and about the UK. The numbers show how much energy is used per person and what each country's **gross national product** is. E is the start of a scattergraph to show these data.

Family carrying firewood

CORE ACTIVITIES

1 Look carefully at the photos **A** to **C**.
  ● Match each of the photos with one of these captions:
    - In many South World countries, poor people often rely on collected firewood for energy.
    - Brazil has to import oil, which is expensive, so many Brazilian cars run on a mixture of petrol and alcohol made from sugar cane grown inside the country.
    - Water can be used to make electricity at dams like the Itaipu Dam on the Parana River.
  ● Suggest two energy uses the family in photo **B** could have for the firewood they have collected.
  ● What do you think gasohol is?
  ● Write a sentence to explain what is meant by **hydro-electric power** (HEP).

C

Petrol station

E

GNP per person (US dollars) vs ENERGY USE per person (million BTUs)

Key:

A = Argentina

Scattergraph

D

E	G	A	S	O	H	O	L	T	K	E
M	T	L	I	L	P	E	H	C	L	S
T	Y	I	Y	L	O	R	T	E	P	R
E	R	E	T	A	W	I	C	N	I	A
N	C	E	G	I	E	T	T	C	E	E
R	K	C	N	A	R	C	A	O	R	L
L	M	D	I	I	S	O	L	A	R	C
P	A	L	C	O	H	O	L	L	W	U
L	F	I	R	E	W	O	O	D	I	N
S	T	E	A	M	O	I	O	A	Y	A
Y	C	M	T	I	L	L	T	B	U	A

Wordsearch

F

COUNTRY	GNP (US Dollars) per person	ENERGY USE (million BTUs) per person
Argentina	1 900	1 800
Brazil	1 500	800
Peru	700	800
Venezuela	2 900	2 900
United Kingdom	5 100	5 200

Poor people use less energy

EXTENSION ACTIVITIES

2 **D** is a wordsearch containing energy words.
- Find as many energy words as you can. (*HINT*: All the energy words in this unit are there - and more as well!)
- Make a table to show renewable and non-renewable types of energy.

3 Study table **F**.
- Write a sentence to explain what gross national product (GNP) is. (HINT: ☞ GLOSSARY.)
- Complete the scattergraph in **E** using the data from **F**.

4 Use your scattergraph to think about this hypothesis:
Countries with a low GNP have low energy use per person - these are South World countries.
- Does your graph lead you to think that the hypothesis is true or not true? Explain your answer.

5 On an outline map of South America, name each of the countries and mark each capital city.
- List the countries not included in table **F**.

6 Think about your decision about the hypothesis in Activity 4.
- Suggest how this decision might be limited because of the number of countries shown on your graph.

7 What types of energy do you use?
- Remember your day so far. Write down a list of energy uses you have made. (HINTS: An alarm clock may use electricity from batteries. Switching on the light uses electricity.
Was there heat on in your home when you got up?)

Targets

* To be aware of the increasing demand for energy in Brazil and of how electric power stations have been developed to satisfy this demand.
* To be concerned about the impact of energy developments on the environment and on people's lives.

A YEAR	ENERGY DEMAND Per person
1940	0.40
1950	0.45
1960	0.55
1970	0.70
1980	0.90
1990 (estimate)	1.15
UNITS ARE TONNES OF OIL EQUIVALENT	

Energy demand in Brazil

As with many developing countries, there has been a growth of demand for energy in Brazil.

Map **B** shows the location of electric power stations in Brazil which have been developed to help satisfy the demand for energy in the country.

However, developing large power stations has impacts on the environment and on local people.

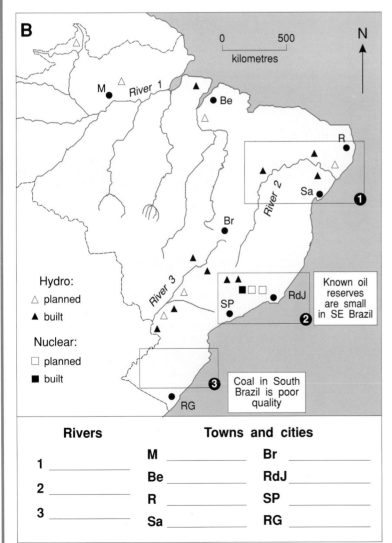

B

Hydro:
△ planned
▲ built

Nuclear:
□ planned
■ built

Known oil reserves are small in SE Brazil

Coal in South Brazil is poor quality

Rivers		Towns and cities	
1 _____		M _____	Br _____
2 _____		Be _____	RdJ _____
3 _____		R _____	SP _____
		Sa _____	RG _____

Power station development in Brazil

CORE ACTIVITIES

1 Look at table **A**.
● Use the data to make a line graph.
● Copy each of these statements about your graph. Next to each statement write if it is true or false.
  - The demand for energy in Brazil is less than it used to be.
  - In 1990 the use of energy was about twice as much as in 1970.

2 Look at map **B**.
● Find out and explain why Brazil has not developed new power stations making electricity from coal or oil.

3 Find a good map of Brazil in your atlas.
● Use it to complete the key to the names of main cities and rivers in Brazil.

4 ☞GLOSSARY.
● Find out and explain how a hydro-electric power station works.
● Make a diagram to show what you have written.

5 Look at photo **C**.
● Suggest what this picture may have to do with hydro-electric power. (*HINT*: Think about flooding.)

C

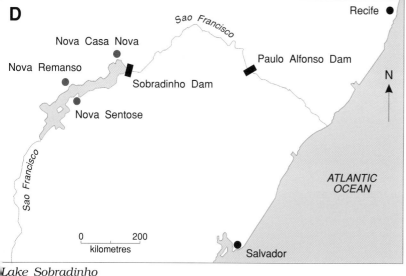

D

Lake Sobradinho

6 Look at map **D**.
 ● Which of the boxes on map **B** does it show, on a larger scale?
 ● Copy and complete:
   The Sobradinho Dam is built on the ____ _____ River. It has created Lake _____ , the largest _____ in South America. The lake is about ____ km long. People who lived on the banks of the river were moved to new villages like ____ ____ _____ .

7 Think about this statement:
The great thing about hydro-electric power is that it is clean. It does not harm the environment. Beautiful lakes are made which harm no one.
 ● Explain what is true and what is false about this statement, and why.

EXTENSION ACTIVITY

8 Electricity can be made in different types of power station (Unit 5.4).
 ● Make a list of four different types.
 ● For each write a short explanation of how it works. (*HINT*: ☞ GLOSSARY.)
 ● Choose one type to research in more detail. Find out about one example of that type.
   - Name your example.
   - Make a location map.
   - Explain why it was developed and the impact it has had on the environment.

5.3 SUGAR CARS

Targets

* To realise that energy sources alternative to those which are accepted (or **conventional**) may be developed.
* To understand that **alternative energy** sources may be economic.
* To make, use and compare pie charts and line graphs.
* To consider the links between sugar-fuelled transport and the environment.

Sugar cars in Rio de Janeiro

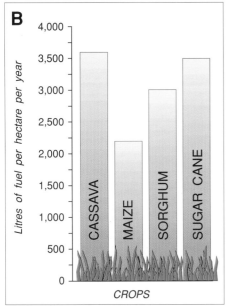
How much alcohol? Four Brazilian crops compared

The conventional energy source for cars is oil. Petrol is made from **refining oil**.

In Brazil many vehicles are fuelled with an alternative form of energy. Alcohol can be distilled from crops including sugar cane, and then blended with petrol.

D explains the reasons behind the development of sugar as an alternative energy source in Brazil, and also shows its effects.

CORE ACTIVITIES

1 Look at photo **A**.
* Copy each of these statements. Next to each statement write down if you think it is true or false.
  - The photo shows the city of Sao Paulo.
  - There seems to be a lot of traffic.
  - Sugar cars look totally different from petrol cars.
  - Brazil's cities only have small roads.

2 Look at graph **B** and its caption.
* Write a sentence to say what graph **B** shows exactly.
* Use graph **B** to complete this table:

Crop	Litres of fuel which could be distilled per **hectare** per year
Cassava	
Maize	
Sorghum	
Sugar cane	

3 Read this hypothesis:
Sugar cane has been used to make fuel in Brazil because it is the crop which can provide the most alcohol per hectare per year.
* Say what do you think of this hypothesis and why.

4 Look at photo **C**.
* Describe the photo as carefully as you can. (*HINT*: Think of what the crop looks like and how densely it is cultivated.)
* Read the caption to photo **C**. Suggest a possible reason for the use of sugar cane rather than cassava for distilling alcohol for cars.

5 Look at the data in **E**.
* Make a series of pie charts to show the percentage of cars made in Brazil which were sugar cars for each of the years between 1980 and 1983.
* Now use the same data to make a line graph.
* Which of the two graphs do you think shows the **trend** in the data best? Why?

*Sugar cane. Huge sugar cane **plantations** have existed in Brazil for hundreds of years.*

D

Around cities food farms have been cleared to grow sugar. Food has to be grown further away and is more expensive.

Brazil uses a lot of cars and lorries because it has a limited railway network.

Sugar fuel is cleaner. It is lead-free and pollution is less.

Sugar cars have created jobs (often badly paid) on sugar cane plantations and in distilleries.

It saves Brazil money on expensive oil imports.

Large areas of rain forest have had to be cleared to plant sugar cane.

A brilliant idea?

6 Refer to your line graph.
- Extend your line graph to estimate the percentage of cars made to use gasohol in 1987. Write down the number your graph predicts.
- The actual figure was 90 per cent. Is that what your graph showed?

7 Read the information in **D**.
- Use it to explain TWO or more economic reasons why sugar cars were thought to be a good idea for Brazil.
- List THREE or more ways sugar cars (good or bad) may affect the environment.
- Suggest ONE reason why the percentage of cars made with sugar power engines fell from 90 per cent in 1988 to about 50 per cent in 1989. (*HINT*: Think about the problems or growing so much sugar cane.)

8 Either:
- Use **D** to explain why, like any development, sugar cars have costs as well as benefits.
- Or: Make a scales diagram to show your view of the balance between costs and benefits of sugar cars.

E YEAR	% OF BRAZILIAN-MADE CARS WHICH WERE SUGAR CARS
1980	22
1981	17
1982	28
1983	47

Sugar cars: made in Brazil

EXTENSION ACTIVITIES

9 You will need an atlas.
- Use your atlas to make a map of Brazil's railway network.
- Mark on your map the locations and names of Brazil's main cities.
- How does your map help explain why 90 per cent of today's Brazilian cars are sugar cars? (*HINT*: Look at **D**.)
- Look back to Unit 4.2. What stage in the model of a developing transport network does Brazil's railway system seem to have reached? Explain your answer.
- Brazil's railway network began at stage 1. What has this to do with Brazil having been a Portuguese colony in the past?

10 Think carefully about this statement:
Sugar cars are a brilliant idea - they should be developed all over the world!
- How much truth is there in the statement?
- List points in favour of the statement and points against.
- Rewrite the statement so that it seems accurate to you.

Targets

* To be aware of the **distribution** of energy resources in the UK.
* To realise the relative importance to the UK of different **primary sources of energy**, and how these may change in the near future.
* To understand what **thermal electricity** is, and how it is generated.

Map **A** shows the distribution of energy resources in the UK, as well as the locations of major electricity power stations.

In the UK people make use of a mix of primary energy sources. Coal is a primary energy source which can be used to generate electricity. This thermal electricity is a **secondary energy source**. Diagram **C** shows how coal can be used to generate electricity in a thermal power station. It also indicates ways in which thermal power stations make an impact on the environment.

A

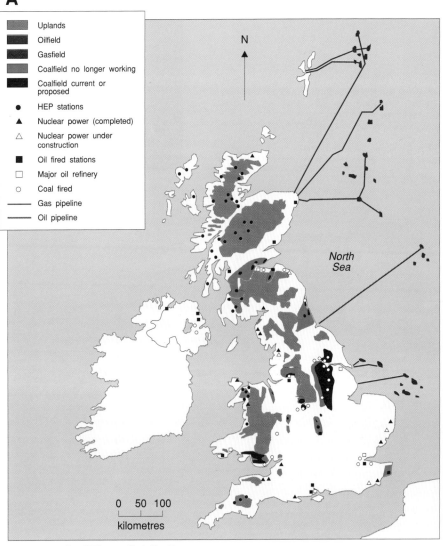

Legend:
- Uplands
- Oilfield
- Gasfield
- Coalfield no longer working
- Coalfield current or proposed
- ● HEP stations
- ▲ Nuclear power (completed)
- △ Nuclear power under construction
- ■ Oil fired stations
- ☐ Major oil refinery
- ○ Coal fired
- Gas pipeline
- Oil pipeline

North Sea

0 50 100
kilometres

Energy in the UK - a distribution map

CORE ACTIVITIES

1 Look at map **A**.
- Read these sentence starts:
  - *Most UK gasfields are below the ...*
  - *UK oilfields are mainly under the ...*
  - *The main current and proposed coalfields are in ...*
  - *Most of the coalfields which are no longer worked are in ...*
- Match each start to one of these ends:
  - *northern North Sea.*
  - *central England.*
  - *north and west Britain.*
  - *southern North Sea.*

2 Using map **A** and an atlas:
- Try to make your own table listing the different types of power station in the UK, with one named example of each.

3 For each type of power station:
- Write one sentence about its distribution.
  EXAMPLE: HEP stations are in the uplands of western Britain. (*HINT*: The sentences in Activity 1 may help you.)

4 Use pie chart **B**:
- To make a table showing the share of the UK's energy which comes from each of the primary sources shown.

5 Look at diagram **C**.
- Write a full explanation of how thermal electricity is generated from coal.
- List three or more impacts of thermal power stations on our environment.

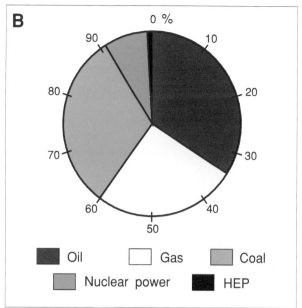

B

| Oil | Gas | Coal |
| Nuclear power | HEP |

Energy use in the UK, 1990

C

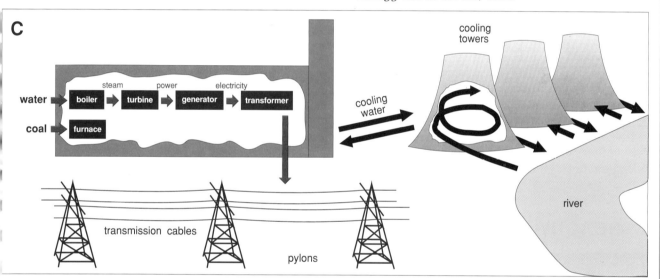

How a thermal power station works

D

PRIMARY ENERGY SOURCE	% OF TOTAL ENERGY USE
Oil	31
Gas	26
Coal	33
Nuclear Power	9
HEP	1

Energy use in the UK, 2000

EXTENSION ACTIVITIES

6 Look at **D**.
- Make a pie chart from the data.
- Compare the pie charts and data for 1990 and 2000.
- Write a few sentences to describe the changes that are expected during the 1990s. (*HINT*: Include how the UK's total energy consumption is expected to change as well as writing about each type.)

7 Think carefully about the sentences you have written for Activity 3.
- Suggest reasons why each type of power station has its own distribution pattern.

5.5 UK CHOICES

Targets

* To be aware that the UK has choices in developing energy.
* To understand the different points of view people hold about energy choices.
* To appreciate the impact on our environment of different energy choices.
* To understand how a **nuclear power** station works.
* To be aware of alternative energy sources that may be developed.

A

Nuclear power station

Developing **nuclear power** is one of the choices the UK has in developing its energy. The development of nuclear power is an issue and people have different views about it.

Some people feel that alternative, renewable sources of energy should be developed. Chart **D** shows some of these, and some of the people in **C** give their views about them. At the moment, alternative renewable energy sources make little contribution to energy development in the UK. The issue is whether they can be developed so that they make a greater contribution.

CORE ACTIVITIES

1 **A** shows a UK nuclear power station.
  ● Draw a sketch of the photo and add these labels:
    - reactor building
    - flat site
    - sea
    - unused land
  ● Use your labels to write two sentences to describe the nuclear power station and its site.

2 Look at diagram **B**.
  ● Explain how a nuclear power station generates electricity.

3 Read the views given by the people in **C**.
  ● Make a table of two columns and use it to record those views which are for the development of more nuclear power in the UK and those which are against.

4 From your table select the views which are about energy and our environment.
  ● Design a diagram or picture to show the possible impacts of energy developments on our environment.
    (*HINT*: You may use more than one image if you wish.)

5 Redraw chart **D**, but put the correct sketch with the correct writing.
  ● Choose one of the alternative energy sources and write an explanation of how it works.
  ● Write a sentence to explain the main advantage of renewable energy. (*HINT*: ☞ GLOSSARY.)
  ● Explain why some people do not think that alternative energy sources are a real choice for the UK.

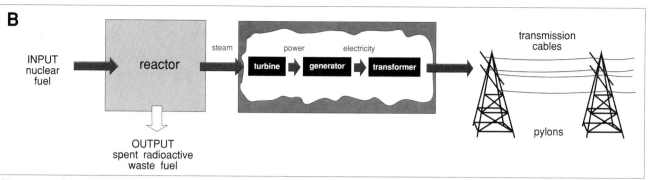

B

How a nuclear power station works

C

> I DON'T THINK NUCLEAR POWER IS SAFE. TERRIBLE ACCIDENTS HAVE HAPPENED

> NUCLEAR POWER IS CLEAN. THERE IS NO POLLUTION LIKE THERE IS FROM A COAL POWER STATION. NUCLEAR POWER DOESN'T INCREASE THE GREENHOUSE EFFECT.

> NUCLEAR FUEL HAS TO BE CONVERTED INTO WASTE WHEN IT HAS BEEN USED UP. IT CAN'T BE DESTROYED - IT JUST HAS TO BE BURIED SOMEWHERE.

> NUCLEAR POWER IS RENEWABLE - NOT LIKE COAL.

> THE UK HAS ENOUGH COAL TO LAST CENTURIES - WE DON'T NEED NUCLEAR POWER.

> WHAT WE NEED ARE ALTERNATIVE, RENEWABLE SOURCES OF ENERGY - LIKE WIND POWER OR SOLAR POWER. THEY DON'T HURT THE ENVIRONMENT.

> THESE ALTERNATIVE ENERGY SOURCES ARE ALL VERY WELL, BUT THEY JUST DON'T MAKE ENOUGH POWER.

Views about energy choices

D

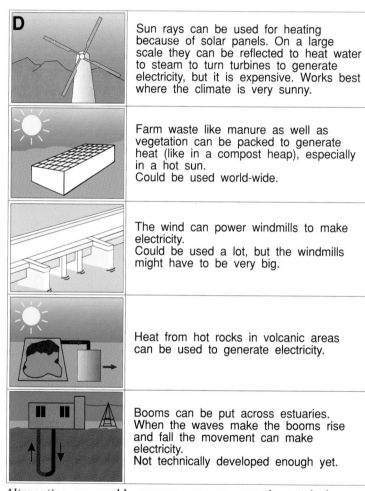

Sun rays can be used for heating because of solar panels. On a large scale they can be reflected to heat water to steam to turn turbines to generate electricity, but it is expensive. Works best where the climate is very sunny.

Farm waste like manure as well as vegetation can be packed to generate heat (like in a compost heap), especially in a hot sun.
Could be used world-wide.

The wind can power windmills to make electricity.
Could be used a lot, but the windmills might have to be very big.

Heat from hot rocks in volcanic areas can be used to generate electricity.

Booms can be put across estuaries. When the waves make the booms rise and fall the movement can make electricity.
Not technically developed enough yet.

Alternative, renewable energy: can you correctly match the pictures and descriptions?

EXTENSION ACTIVITY

6 What are your views about nuclear power and alternative renewable sources of energy?
- For each, draw a scales diagram to show the balance of your views.
- Explain why you hold these views.
  (*HINT*: Look at the views for and against before you decide.)

6.1 WORK IS...

Targets

* To understand what we mean by work.
* To realise that not all work is paid.

What is work? Photos **A** to **C** may help you to decide.

Ruth's morning involves work which is paid and work which is not paid. Jobs are paid work, but much useful work is unpaid. This does not mean that work which is unpaid is less useful. A lot of work, paid as well as unpaid, but especially unpaid, is done by women like Ruth.

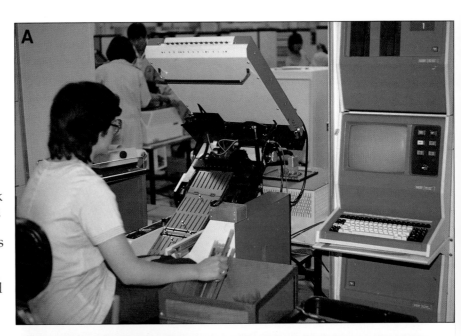

CORE ACTIVITIES

1 Look at photos **A** to **C**.
* Complete this table about what you see

Photo	Activity	Job	Useful work?
A	Working in a factory	Yes	Yes
B			
C			

2 Here is a list of some more activities:
   Farming
   Cleaning your home
   Cleaning someone else's home
   Writing a book
   Playing tennis
   Typing
   Mending your car
   Mending someone else's car
* Make a table like the one in Activity 1 to show if you think each activity is a job and if you think each activity is work.
* Which of the activities are unpaid? Are these work? Explain your answer.

3 Read about Ruth's morning (**D**).
- Write down the activities which are paid and those which are unpaid.
- Now list the activities which you think are work and those which are not.
- Make a pie chart to show how time is shared out over Ruth's morning. Your pie chart will need three sections:
    - Time doing paid work
    - Time doing unpaid work
    - Time not working.
  (*HINT*: Ruth's morning is 6 hours long, so first split the circle into six parts of 1 hour each.)

4 Think about these endings to the sentence starting **Work is** ...
  ... having a job.
  ... helping other people.
  ... activities which are not leisure.
  ... always paid.
  ... making things.
- For each ending, write down if you agree, partly agree or disagree and then explain why.
- What would your ending be to the sentence starting *Work is ...?*
  (*HINT*: It may be one of those above, but could well be something different.)

Ruth's morning

5 Using magazines or newspapers:
- Make a collection of pictures showing work which is paid and work which is unpaid.

6 Talk to a woman you know about her morning.
- Make a pie chart for her morning, like that which you made for Activity 3. (*HINT*: She could be someone at home, or a teacher, or just someone you know.)
- Make a pie chart for your morning.
- Compare the three pie charts you now have. Describe the ways they are similar and the ways they are different.

Targets

* To realise that a new **industrial** development can provide jobs in an area where they are needed.
* To be aware of the factors which a company may think about in choosing a new **location** for a factory.

The Nissan car factory at Sunderland is a major modern industrial development in the north-east of England.

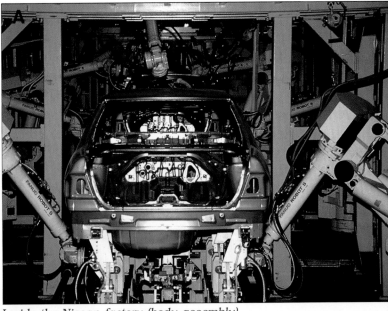

Inside the Nissan factory (body assembly)

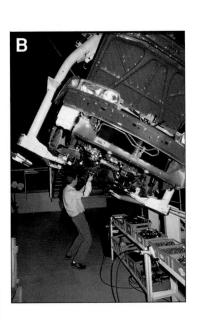

Inside the Nissan factory (final assembly)

CORE ACTIVITIES

1 Look at photos **A** and **B**.
* Copy each of these statements. Next to each write if it is true or false.
  - Photo **A** shows many people at work on car bodies.
  - This could be a noisy environment for work.
  - Photo **B** shows that the final assembly of cars still relies on people's skills.
  - There is plenty of space for people to work in on the factory floor.

2 Study map **C**.
* Use it to complete this table about factors such as, **communications** and **labour supply** which Nissan took into account when choosing the location of their factory:

Factor	Map evidence
Communications	
Labour supply	

The north-east of England had a lot of unemployment. Traditional industries like coal mining, shipbuilding and **heavy engineering** had been declining for many years. The Nissan factory was welcomed by many local people because it provided jobs - over 3 500 jobs by 1992.

North-east England

3 Two factors which influenced Nissan's decision to locate in Sunderland were:
- The British government gave money to firms wanting to develop factories in the north-east of England.
- The site used to be an airfield - it was large, flat and not already built on.
● Why do you think the government would help firms to develop factories in regions like the north-east of England?
● List three advantages of the chosen site itself.
● Why is such a site important for a car factory?

4 Read the comments made in **D**.
● Write down another two factors which were important to Nissan in deciding to develop the factory at Sunderland.
● Why did some people object to the building of the car factory at Sunderland?
● What answer do you think a person living in Sunderland and looking for a job might give?

EXTENSION ACTIVITIES

5 Think about this statement:
When a company chooses a new location to develop a factory there are many factors to consider.
● Write about each of the factors which Nissan considered.
● Explain how each one was important in the company's decision to develop at Sunderland.

6 Look back to Unit 1.5.
● Complete a development profile for the Nissan factory. (*HINT*: Allow space to add more costs and benefits after you have studied Unit 6.3.)

D

One of the main attractions for Nissan was local enthusiasm. Lots of people from the area were very keen on the development.

Car factories in other parts of the country could suffer if Nissan succeed.

Nissan will employ thousands of people with a no-strike agreement and good working conditions. That's good news all round.

Different views

6.3 BEYOND THE FACTORY

Targets

* To realise the effects of a major new industrial development on the region around it.
* To consider the impact of industrial development on our environment.
* To analyse the pattern of industrial development by Japanese companies and their subsidiaries in the UK.

The Nissan factory is a development which has brought jobs to the north-east of England. There have also been effects on the development of the region beyond the factory itself. We sometimes call these spin-off effects.

The Nissan development has also had an environmental impact.

The Sunderland Nissan factory is one of a number of recent industrial developments in the UK. Photo **D** shows another north-east development - the Metrocentre out-of-town shopping complex near Gateshead. It is the largest such shopping development in Europe and is located 12 km from the Nissan factory.

A THE NISSAN FACTORY HAS HAD A NUMBER OF SPIN-OFFS. A FACTORY HAS OPENED IN NEARBY WASHINGTON TO MAKE CAR SEATS. THE OLD DUNLOP TYRE WORKS HAS BEEN TAKEN OVER BY A JAPANESE FIRM TO MAKE TYRES FOR NISSAN, AND AN ENGINEERING FIRM HAS JOINED WITH NISSAN TO MAKE ENGINE COMPONENTS.

INDIRECT SPIN-OFFS HERE INCLUDED:-
1. CLOSE LINKS WITH LOCAL UNIVERSITIES AND POLYTECHNICS TO HELP RESEARCH AND SUPPLY TRAINED STAFF.
2. SMALL BUSINESSES HAVE GROWN. FOR EXAMPLE, A LOCAL PRINTER WHO MAKES BROCHURES FOR NISSAN HAS OPENED A NEW FACTORY TO SUPPLY THEM.

Spin-offs

CORE ACTIVITIES

1 Cars are assembled from many different parts, or **components**.
  * Write a list of car components and what they are made of.
    EXAMPLES: windscreen - glass
    steering wheel - plastic
    body - steel.
  * Try for a list of at least ten.

2 Look at **A**.
  * Write down three industrial developments which supply components to the Nissan factory.
  * Write a few sentences about the spin-off effects of the Nissan development. (*HINT*: For each spin-off, describe what it is and explain the connection to the Nissan factory.)

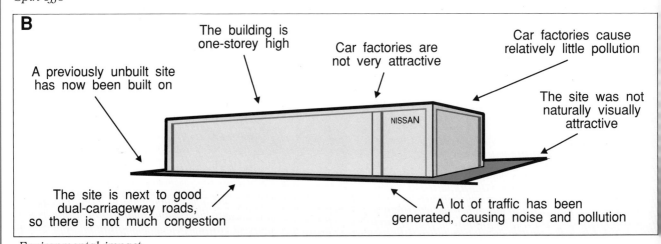

B

The building is one-storey high

Car factories are not very attractive

Car factories cause relatively little pollution

A previously unbuilt site has now been built on

The site was not naturally visually attractive

The site is next to good dual-carriageway roads, so there is not much congestion

A lot of traffic has been generated, causing noise and pollution

Environmental impact

3 Look at photo **D**.
  ● Suggest how the Metrocentre and Nissan developments may be linked. (*HINT*: Think of how the Metrocentre might have helped attract Nissan to the region, and of how its shops might benefit from the Nissan workers.)

4 Look at diagram **B** and think about this statement:
  'The Nissan development has had no effect at all on the local environment.'
  ● Do you agree, partly agree or disagree with this statement? Give reasons for your opinion. (*HINT*: Try to use each of the diagram labels.)

5 Look at map **C**.
  ● Describe the distribution of industrial development in the UK made by Japanese companies and their subsidiaries. (*HINT*: Look for regions where there are a lot, e.g. central Scotland and regions where there are just a few, e.g. Northern Ireland.)
  ● Try to think of one reason behind the pattern you have described: (*HINT*: The British government offers help to companies which might think about developing factories in areas of higher than average unemployment.)

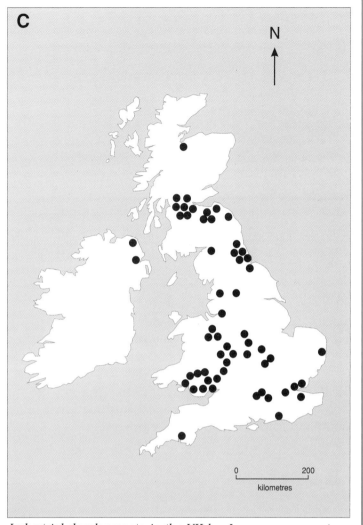

C

Industrial developments in the UK by Japanese companies and their subsidiaries.

Metrocentre shopping complex, Gateshead

EXTENSION ACTIVITIES

6 Refer back to Unit 6.2.
  ● Complete the development profile of the Nissan factory which you began in Unit 6.2.

7 Think of an industrial development you know.
  ● Complete a development profile for it. Include its impact on the local environment.

Targets

* To realise that big car companies are often multinational.
* To understand how a major new industrial development may not be good for jobs.
* To appreciate that some multinational companies may be more powerful than some governments.

Nissan is a multinational company, based in Japan, but making and selling cars in many different countries. Two of these countries are the UK (Unit 6.2) and Malaysia.

In Malaysia, Nissan sell far fewer cars than they used to. One of the main reasons has been competition from a new car made in Malaysia and called the Proton Saga.

People have different views about the Proton Saga and about the role of the Japanese multinational company Mitsubishi in its development.

A

A Proton car. The factory that builds the Proton Saga was developed with money lent by the Japanese company Mitsubishi.

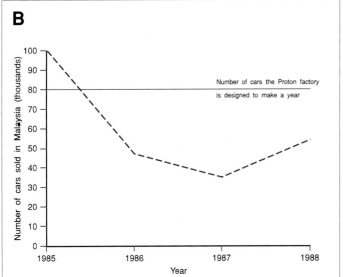

B

Number of cars sold in Malaysia (thousands)

Number of cars the Proton factory is designed to make a year

1985   1986   1987   1988
Year

The Malaysian car market

Number of jobs

7,000 6,000 5,000 4,000 3,000 2,000 1,000   0   1,000 2,000

Jobs created by the Proton development

Jobs lost because of the Proton development

(Other car companies could not compete with Proton's subsidised cheap prices as the market shrank.)

Malaysian population = 15 million people

■ 1% of Malaysians drive a car

CORE ACTIVITIES

1 Look at **A** and read the caption.
  ● Who lent the money to start the Proton car factory?
  ● Why do you think the Malaysian government wanted to develop a car factory? (*HINT*: Think back to Unit 6.3.)

2 Find a good map of the Far East in your atlas.
  ● On a copy of map **C**, complete the names of the seas and countries.
  ● Make a key to name the capital cities. (*HINT*: Each letter is the first letter of the city name.)

3 Study the line graph in **B**.
- Copy and complete:
  In 1985 the number of cars sold in Malaysia was about _____ . The next year this fell by about half to _____ and in 1987 fell again to _____ . In 1988 there was a rise in sales to about _____ .
- The Proton car was on sale from late 1985 onwards. How well do you think it sold?
- Use the other graphs in **B** to collect the following data:
  - the number of cars a year the Proton factory can make
  - the number of jobs lost in the Malaysian car industry while the Proton factory has been working
  - the percentage of people in Malaysia who drive cars.

4 Read the views people give about the Proton car development.
- Make a costs and benefits table. (*HINT*: Use the views in **D**, facts from the rest of this unit and any other costs or benefits you might be able to think of.)
- Draw a scales diagram to show if you feel the costs outweighed the benefits, or the other way round.

5 Think about this statement:
Multinational companies can be more powerful than governments.
- Do you agree, partly agree or disagree with this statement? Explain how the story of the Proton development helps you reach this view.

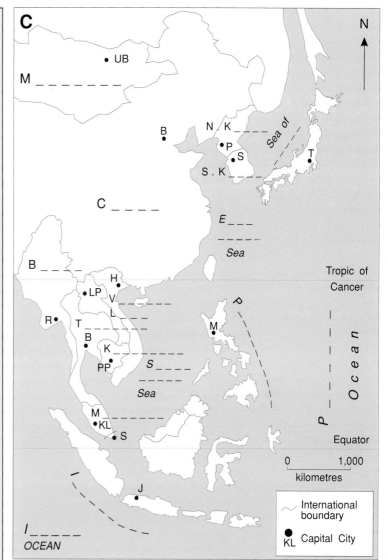

The Far East

6 Imagine a television discussion programme about the Proton development. You are the presenter.
- What questions would you ask the people in **D**?
- What do you think would be their likely replies? (*HINT*: Write your answer like a script.)

D

THE PROTON SAGA IS MALAYSIA'S NATIONAL CAR. IT ADDS TO OUR PRESTIGE ABROAD.

THE FACTORY IS VERY MODERN AND MECHANISED.

IT'S BEEN A GREAT SUCCESS. IT SELLS MORE IN MALAYSIA THAN ANY OTHER CAR AND IS NOW BEING EXPORTED TO THE UK.

NOT MANY MALAYSIANS WORK THERE. THE GOVERNMENT SHOULD HAVE USED THE MONEY IT SPENT ON SMALLER FACTORIES WHERE PEOPLE WOULD GET JOBS.

THE FACTORY IS NOW OWNED BY THE JAPANESE - MALAYSIA HAS BECOME EVEN MORE DEPENDENT ON OUTSIDERS.

THE PROTON SAGA HAS COST MALAYSIA A FORTUNE. THE MONEY COULD HAVE BEEN BETTER SPENT ON DEVELOPING PUBLIC TRANSPORT FOR EVERYONE TO USE.

Views about the Proton Saga

6.5 CAR WORLD

Targets

* To realise that most world cars are made by a few American, Japanese and European multinational companies.
* To be aware of the costs of the world continuing to make more and more cars, including costs to the environment.
* To question if cars are a good transport industry for South World countries to develop.

Car making is the biggest industry in the world's economy. Cars make up about 12 per cent of the value of industrial goods sold in the world.

Four out of every five cars are made by multinational companies.

Table **B** shows the number of cars made in the world between 1950 and 1990. The development of the car-making industry has had benefits for people. However, there have also been costs for people and for the environment.

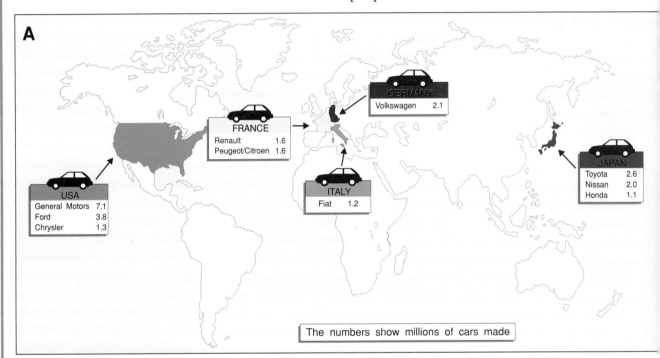

A

GERMANY
Volkswagen 2.1

FRANCE
Renault   1.6
Peugeot/Citroen 1.6

USA
General Motors 7.1
Ford   3.8
Chrysler   1.3

ITALY
Fiat   1.2

JAPAN
Toyota   2.6
Nissan   2.0
Honda   1.1

The numbers show millions of cars made

Top ten car multinationals: some facts

CORE ACTIVITIES

1 Look at map **A**.
  ● Summarise the facts in a table like this:

Multinational company	Home country	Millions of cars made
General Motors	USA	7.1
Ford		

2 Now look carefully at your summary table.
  ● Which three parts of the world are home to the top ten car multinationals?
  ● Are these in the North or in the South World?

3 Look at the data in table **B**.
  ● Draw a line graph to show the change in the number of cars made in the world between 1950 and 1990.
  ● Describe what your graph shows about this change. (*HINT*: Include whether there are more or fewer cars made; how big the change has been; whether the change has been at the same rate or not.)

B Year	**Cars made** (millions)
1950	8
1960	13
1970	23
1980	28
1990 (estimate)	31

World car production

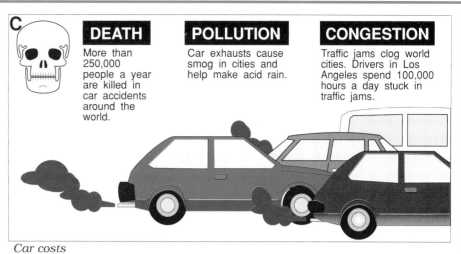

DEATH
More than 250,000 people a year are killed in car accidents around the world.

POLLUTION
Car exhausts cause smog in cities and help make acid rain.

CONGESTION
Traffic jams clog world cities. Drivers in Los Angeles spend 100,000 hours a day stuck in traffic jams.

Car costs

D Wages paid to car workers

Country	US dollars per hour
USA	19.88
West Germany	16.91
Canada	13.45
Sweden	12.75
Japan	11.97
France	11.22
Italy	10.55
Australia	9.56
UK	8.66
Mexico	2.66
Taiwan	2.24
Korea	1.90
Brazil	1.72

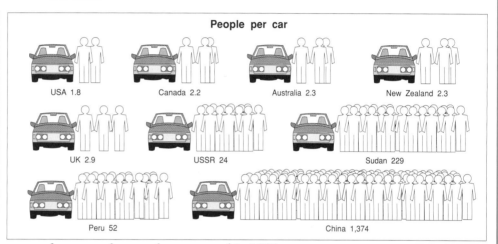

People per car

USA 1.8 · Canada 2.2 · Australia 2.3 · New Zealand 2.3
UK 2.9 · USSR 24 · Sudan 229
Peru 52 · China 1,374

Comparing North and South: wages for car workers and car ownership 1986

EXTENSION ACTIVITY

4 What are your feelings about cars and the environment?
- Design a poster to express them. The job of the poster is to draw attention to the costs for the environment of making more and more cars. (*HINT*: Use **C** to help. Make your poster eye-catching.)
- Make a table to show the costs and benefits of the development of the world car industry. (*HINT*: **C** will help you find costs. Try to think of the benefits yourself. Thinking about jobs and ease of moving around would be a good start.)

5 Study chart **D**.
- Think about these hypotheses:
  Car workers are paid equally well all over the world.
  In North World countries, there is a higher level of car ownership than in countries of the South World.
  Multinational companies develop car factories in the South World because the people there buy a lot of cars.
- For each hypothesis, write down if you think it is true, partly true or untrue. Explain your decision.

6 You are a citizen of a city in the South World - perhaps Kuala Lumpur, the capital of Malaysia. You have heard that a multinational car company intends to develop a factory in your city with your government's help. Discussing the idea with a friend, you find she disagrees with you.
- What could the conversation between you be like? Write down what you think you would each say, and try to make it include as many good and bad points of the development as you can. (*HINT*: Use Units 6.2 to 6.5 for ideas.)

Targets

* To find out the names of the main geographical features of Peru.
* To be aware of the contrasting environments found in Peru.
* To consider how we present and react to images of a country.

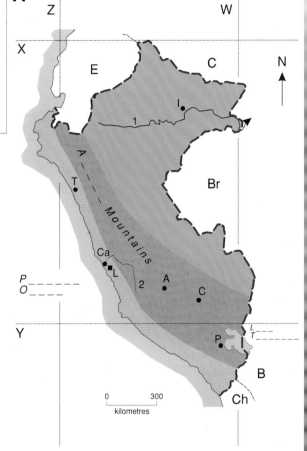

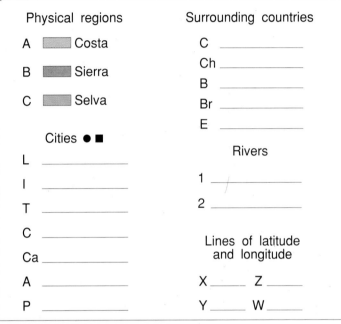

Physical regions

A ▢ Costa

B ▢ Sierra

C ▢ Selva

Cities ● ■

L _____

I _____

T _____

C _____

Ca _____

A _____

P _____

Surrounding countries

C _____

Ch _____

B _____

Br _____

E _____

Rivers

1 _____

2 _____

Lines of latitude and longitude

X _____ Z _____

Y _____ W _____

The main geographical features of Peru

Peru is a country in the South World and is located on the western side of South America. In Peru there are three main physical regions with contrasting types of climate. Like other countries, including Britain, Peru is a very varied place where people have many different occupations.

B REGION	MONTH	J	F	M	A	M	J	J	A	S	O	N	D
A	TEMP (°C)	21	22	23	21	17	15	14	14	15	16	17	19
A	RAINFALL (mm)	1	1	1	1	1	1	4	7	5	2	1	1
B	TEMP (°C)	26	26	25	25	26	25	25	24	27	27	26	26
B	RAINFALL (mm)	280	250	280	170	140	40	70	60	70	120	130	300
C	TEMP (°C)	12	12	12	11	10	9	8	10	12	12	12	12
C	RAINFALL (mm)	130	120	110	50	20	10	5	20	30	70	70	90

Three climates

Images of Peru

CORE ACTIVITIES

1 Look at map **A**.
  ● On a copy of the map complete the labelling and the key. (*HINT*: Use the contents page of your atlas to help you find the most suitable maps of South America.)
  ● Use your map and key to complete this description: Peru lies between Chile and _____ on the _____ Ocean coast of South America. The country stretches from a latitude of about _____ °S as far north as _____ . Its capital city is Lima, which is some _____ km across the _____ Mountains from the Brazilian border in the east.

2 Using the data in **B**:
  ● Complete climate graphs of the three physical regions of Peru.

3 Look at the photos in **C**.
  ● Write a detailed description of what they show you about Peru. (*HINT*: Think about people as well as the physical environment.)

EXTENSION ACTIVITIES

4 Think about your description of Peru from Activity 3.
  ● Use other sources to collect more varied images of Peru. (*HINT*: Use travel brochures as well as books and magazines.)

5 Think about Britain.
  ● Write a unit called 'This is Britain', including a map, climate data for different regions and just six photos.
  ● How well have you presented an image of variety in Britain? What else would you like to have included?

7.2 POPULATION AND DEVELOPMENT

* To understand the pattern of development in Peru.
* To look for links between population growth and the development of Peru.

Peru's development has been going on for many centuries. The drawing below shows some highlights of the country's long history. These may in turn help to explain its pattern of population growth.

A

FROM 1948 PERU BEGAN TO DEVELOP INDUSTRIES, MOSTLY USING MONEY FROM ABROAD.
BUT EVEN TODAY MANY PERUVIANS REMAIN AS POOR PEASANTS WITH NO LAND OF THEIR OWN. A LOT OF THEM STILL WORK ON THE OLD HACIENDAS FOR BIG LANDOWNERS. THERE IS MUCH MIGRATION TO THE CITIES, ESPECIALLY TO LIMA, IN SEARCH OF JOBS IN INDUSTRY AND IN CITY SERVICES.

THOUSANDS OF YEARS BEFORE THE INCAS, CIVILISATIONS FLOURISHED IN PERU. OVER 20,000 YEARS AGO THE MOCHICAN PEOPLE BUILT PALACES IN THE COASTAL DESERT

BY 1600, WITH PERU A COLONY IN THE SPANISH EMPIRE, 2 MILLION AMERINDIAN PEOPLE HAD DIED AFTER BEING FORCED TO MINE GOLD, SILVER AND MERCURY FOR THE SPANIARDS. HUNGER AND DISEASE HAD BECOME COMMONPLACE. RICH SPANIARDS SEIZED LARGE ESTATES (HACIENDAS) TO FARM USING SLAVES BROUGHT FROM AFRICA.

THE INCA CIVILISATION DOMINATED PERU IN 1450. THE INCA RULERS LIVED WELL FROM THE LABOURS OF POORER AMERINDIANS UNDER THEIR COMMAND, BUT THERE WERE FOOD AND JOBS FOR ALL. HUGE IRRIGATION SYSTEMS WERE DESIGNED TO BRING MELTWATERS FROM THE HIGH ANDES TO IRRIGATE FIELDS.

IN 1532 THE SPANISH CONQUEST BEGAN. SPANISH CONQUISTADORS MURDERED THE INCA KING ATAHUALPA AND HUNDREDS OF ORDINARY AMERINDIANS.

IN 1821 PERU BECAME INDEPENDENT AND LEFT THE SPANISH EMPIRE
BY 1848 PERU'S ECONOMY WAS BASED ON EXPORTING MINERALS AND GUANO (BIRD DROPPINGS) USED AS FERTILISER BUT MOST OF THE MONEY DID NOT GO TO ORDINARY PERUVIANS.
IN 1883 PERU LOST THE PACIFIC WAR A FEW RICH FAMILIES REBUILT THE COUNTRY'S ECONOMY BY EXPORTING SUGAR, COTTON, WOOL, RUBBER, COPPER AND OIL. MINERAL AND OIL COMPANIES WERE OWNED BY BIG FIRMS FROM THE USA.

Peru's development through history

Machu Picchu - ruined city of the Incas

C	BC		AD											
YEAR	400	200	600	1000	1200	1400	1500	1600	1700	1800	1850	1900	1950	2000
POPULATION (millions) (often estimated)	0.6	0.7	1.1	1.5	1.7	1.8	2.0	1.5	1.5	1.5	2.0	3.75	8.0	27.0

Population growth data

CORE ACTIVITIES

1 The boxes in diagram **A** are not in the correct order.
   - Work out the correct order and then write an account of the historical development of Peru in your own words.

2 Look carefully at photo **B**.
   - Write a description of what you can see in the photo. (*HINT*: Think about the shape of the land, the weather and the evidence of human use.)
   - What is Machu Picchu?
   - Why is it a difficult place to build a city?
   - What could be the reason for siting Machu Picchu so high?
   - The Incas were supplied by food grown on mountainside **terraces**. Explain what these terraces were or make a diagram to show why they were needed. (*HINT*: ☞ GLOSSARY. Think about **surface run-off** and **soil erosion**.)

3 Look at the data in table **C**.
   - Plot a large line graph of the population growth of Peru.
   - On your graph add labels to show the dates of the main events in Peru's history.
     EXAMPLE: Use an arrow to label 1532 'The Spanish Conquest begins'.
   - Describe the trends shown by your graph. (*HINT*: Think about periods when the population grew quickly, grew slowly and shrank.)
   - Write a few sentences to link historical events with the trends you have described.

EXTENSION ACTIVITIES

4 Use other sources to find out more about the Incas and their way of life.
   - Write a short talk for a group of tourists who are visiting Machu Picchu.

5 Peru's population has grown significantly since 1400.
   - Design and draw a graph to show changes in the rate of growth of Peru's population between 1400 and 2000. Use 50-year intervals.

7.3 MIGRATION

Targets

* To understand the changing pattern of migration in Peru.
* To make and use a **choropleth map**.

People who move home from one place to another are migrants. Migration in Peru is an important aspect of the country's development, and the pattern of migration is a changing one.

The main type of internal migration in Peru is rural-urban migration (moving from the countryside to the towns). Table **B** gives information about migration from the different departments of Peru (map **C**) to the **capital city** of Lima.

There are rural-urban migrants in Peru who are going to live in other towns and cities in the country, not just Lima. These towns include Piura, Chiclayo, Arequipa, Iquitos, Cuzco, Huancayo and Trujillo. The locations of these towns are also shown by map **C**.

Some Peruvians have moved from the countryside to their nearest big town, and then on to Lima later. This is two-stage migration.

A part of Lima - city of migrants?

B DEPARTMENT		% OF POPULATION MIGRATING TO LIMA
Name	Map Key Number	
Amazonas	1	9
Ancash	2	25
Apurimac	3	32
Arequipa	4	15
Ayacucho	5	32
Cajamarca	6	11
Cuzco	7	10
Huancavelica	8	19
Huanuco	9	15
Ica	10	23
Junin	11	18
La Libertad	12	13
Lambayeque	13	12
Lima Metro	14	-
Lima Rest	15	34
Loreto	16	9
Madre de Dios	17	9
Moquegua	18	8
Pasco	19	19
Piura	20	10
Puno	21	6
San Martin	22	9
Tacna	23	6
Tumbes	24	11
Ucayali	25	6

Migration to Lima: data

CORE ACTIVITIES

1 Look at photo **A**.
● Either write a description or make a labelled sketch of what you see. Use these words:
   bus
   shanty
   steep hillside
   shop
   garage
   crowded
   rubbish.
● Write sentences on what photo **A** tells you about:
   - living conditions in Lima
   - how migrants might reach Lima and how they might feel on arrival

2 Match each of these migration words to its correct meaning:
Migration means people moving inside the country.
Migrant means people migrating from countryside to town.
Internal migration means moving to a new place to live.
Rural-urban migration means moving to one town and then on to another town later.
Two-stage migration means a person who moves somewhere new to live.
EXAMPLE: Migration means moving to a new place to live.

C

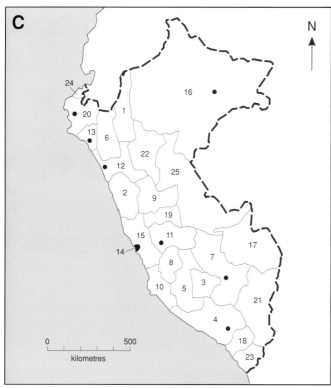

Migration to Lima (the numbers refer to the departments of Peru and the red lines show their boundary)

D

Period	Migration type
In Inca times (before the Spanish colonisation)	It is known that it was not unusual for people to move from one part of the Inca Empire to another.
Spanish colonial times (sixteenth to early nineteeth centuries)	Local Amerindians were often forced to move to work in the Spanish-owned mines.
After independence in 1820	Men would commonly migrate seasonally to work in the mines and in plantations (e.g. sugar) in irrigated parts of the coastal desert. Their families often moved with them to settle permanently.
The late twentieth century (1950 onwards)	As Peru's population has increased, people have increasingly left the country-side to live in cities, especially Lima. Many migrants live in shanty towns in family groups. Lima attracts more women migrants than men.

Changes to migration in Peru

3 Look at the data in table **B**.
- Shade in a copy of map **C** and make a **choropleth map** of migration to Lima. Add a key. (*HINT*: Choose shadings which become denser or darker as the figures increase.)
- Use your choropleth map to describe the pattern of migration to Lima. (*HINT*: Look for where most and fewest people are from. Are they from close or far away? Are they from the desert region, the mountains or the rain forest?)

4 You will need an atlas.
- Use the index page of your atlas to name the Peruvian towns located on map **C**. Make a key for their names.

5 People move from the countryside to the towns because of push and pull factors.
- Explain what these factors are and give some examples. (HINT: ☞ GLOSSARY and look back to Unit 3.4.)

6 Look at **D**.
- Describe, in your own words, how the pattern of migration in Peru has been changing.

EXTENSION ACTIVITY

7 Think about this statement:
- Internal migration in Peru is a new thing - it involves mainly young males moving from the countryside straight to the capital.
- Do you agree with the ideas in this statement? Explain your reasons carefully. (*HINT*: Deal with one idea at a time. There are four in the statement.)

7.4 A VALLEY IN THE ANDES

Targets

* To understand the land use and settlement patterns which are developing in an area in Peru.
* To find out how people's occupations in the area are affected by the environment.
* To outline the distribution of population in Peru.

The Vilcanota Valley is in eastern Peru. Its river flows north from its source in the High Andes and is a tributary of the Ucayali whose waters help feed the River Amazon.

Map **A** shows the settlement pattern of the valley. It also contains information about the

A

Town
Railway
Main roads

N

R. Ucayali

Bolgnesi

Atalaya

R. Urubamba

R. Tambo

ANDES

R. Vilcanota

Camisea

Quillabamba

Urubamba

Calca

Urcas

Cuzco

Sicuani

Urubamba Valley leads on to the valley of the Ucayali River and down into the Amazon Rain Forest. Here there is lumbering.

Vilcanota Valley occupations are chiefly agricultural. Crops of maize and fruit on flood plains and livestock on lower slopes. Subsistence farming on upper slopes.

Cuzco and other towns provide some industrial and service employment. Tourism to Machu Picchu provides some work in Cuzco.

Population distribution in Peru

Chiclaya

Lima Callao

Arequipa

Very low density → Very high density

0   100
kilometres

The Vilcanota and Urubamba Valley

occupations of the people who live there. The inset shows the distribution of population in Peru.

Because the Andes Mountains are so high, the climate changes considerably from the lower slopes to the summits. As a result, a series of land-use zones can be seen up the valley side.

CORE ACTIVITIES

1 Look at **A**.
- Copy and complete this introduction to the Vilcanota and Urubamba Valley:
  The Vilcanota and Urubamba are _____ flowing in a steep-sided valley in the _____ Mountains of _____ Peru. The rivers flow _____ from _____ of Sicuani to _____ where the Urubamba is joined by the _____ and becomes the _____ river.

  Use these words:
  Andes   Ucayali   south
  Tambo north   rivers   eastern
  Atalaya

2 Read these statements about the settlement pattern in the valley:
  Most of the settlements are near the rivers.
  Some settlements are built on high ground, perhaps for defensive reasons.
  The towns are well linked by road and rail.
  The density of settlement increases downstream.
  The settlement pattern is linear (in a line).
- Which are true and which are false?
- Use the true statements to describe and explain the settlement pattern.

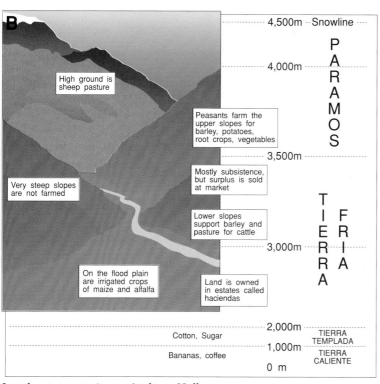

B

4,500m -- Snowline -----	P A R A M O S
4,000m -----	
High ground is sheep pasture	
Peasants farm the upper slopes for barley, potatoes, root crops, vegetables	
3,500m -----	T I E R R A F R I A
Very steep slopes are not farmed	
Mostly subsistence, but surplus is sold at market	
Lower slopes support barley and pasture for cattle	
3,000m -----	
On the flood plain are irrigated crops of maize and alfalfa	
Land is owned in estates called haciendas	
2,000m -----	
Cotton, Sugar	TIERRA TEMPLADA
1,000m -----	
Bananas, coffee	TIERRA CALIENTE
0 m	

Land-use zones in an Andean Valley

C WHAT'S LAND REFORM FOR?
IT'S SUPPOSED TO HAVE DONE AWAY WITH HACIENDAS AND REPLACED THEM WITH CO-OPERATIVES SO EVERYONE COULD SHARE THE WORK - AND THE PROFITS. WELL, IT'S WORKED FOR SOME, I SUPPOSE, BUT IT STILL DOESN'T INVOLVE EVERYBODY.

YOU SEE WHAT HAPPENED WAS THAT THE LAND WAS SHARED BETWEEN THE PEOPLE WHO WORKED FOR THE HACIENDA FULL TIME. MOST PEASANTS DIDN'T - THEY MIGHT HAVE AT BUSY TIMES LIKE HARVEST, BUT THE REST OF THE TIME THEY DIDN'T. SO THEY GOT NOTHING.

THAT'S CAUSED ILL-FEELING, ANGER AND TROUBLE. SOME CO-OPERATIVES HAVE EVEN BEEN ATTACKED BY GUERRILLAS. THEN NOBODY IS ANY BETTER OFF. IF ONLY IT HAD BEEN DONE PROPERLY AT THE START!

Land reform in the Andes

Traditionally, the land of the Sierra was organised into large estates called haciendas which were owned by rich landowners. This was a system left over from Spanish colonial times. Now much of the land has been reorganised into cooperatives owned and run by groups of local peasants (Campesinos). The progress of this development is explained by Bautista, a Campesino, in **C**, above.

3 Look carefully at **B**.
- How is the land owned in the valley?
- How are steep and high ground used?
- Give three reasons why maize can be grown on the flood plain.
- What is the height and land use of the Paramos zone?
- Why do you think the peasants farm the upper slopes for themselves?

4 Using **A**:
- Complete this table about occupations in the Vilcanota and Urubamba Valley:

Locations	Occupations	Environment
1. Cuzco and other towns	Industry and service jobs. Tourism.	Urban. Inca remains.
2. Vilcanota Valley (lower slopes)		

- Use the inset to map **A**, to write a description and explanation of the distribution of population in Peru. (*HINT*: Remember the three different physical regions of Peru and what you know of the country's past. Look back at Unit 7.2.)

5 Look at **C**.
- Write sentences to explain each of these:
  - land reform
  - hacienda

6 Read what Bautista says about land reform in the Sierra. As a television journalist you have been assigned to interview him to find out what the land reform development has been about and whether as an ordinary Peruvian he feels it has been successful.
- Prepare your questions. What do you expect his answers to be?

EXTENSION ACTIVITY

7 The Vilcanota and Urubamba Valley does not cross the coastal region of Peru.
- Make a map of the coastal desert region, use **A** as a guide.
- Research information about occupations and land use in the coastal zone, and use this to annotate your map.

Targets

* To decide what characteristics of development a South World country might show.
* To find out how far Peru displays these characteristics.
* To use and make a scattergraph.

Peru is a developing country of the South World. What characteristics of development do such countries show? How far does Peru display these characteristics?

By looking closely at the information on these pages you may be able to answer these questions.

A Development Characteristics	Expected Score	ACTUAL SCORE	
		Peru	Control
Infant mortality (under 5 years old)			
Life expectancy			
Illiteracy (unable to read and write)			
TV ownership			
Access to telephones			
Car ownership			
Railway density			
% of people aged under 15 years			
Income per person (average)			

Development characteristics

CORE ACTIVITIES

1 Read the list of development characteristics in **A**.
 * Decide if you would expect Peru to score high, average or low (compared with other countries of the world). Use scores from 1 to 5 (lowest to highest) and enter your decisions on a copy of **A**, in the column headed 'Expected score'.

2 Study the data in **B**.
 * Enter the actual scores for Peru's development characteristics in the next column of your copy of **A**.
 * How correct were your expectations? Which were right, which too high and which too low? Which score (if any) surprises you most?

3 Now complete the 'Control' column. The scores in this column represent the control against which you can compare Peru's characteristics of development.
 * Complete the column by choosing one of the following options:
  - the scores for a single North World country
  - the average score for the countries shown
  - the score for the most developed country in each case

B DEVELOPMENT CHARACTERISTIC SCORE (1-5 LOW-HIGH)	Country							
	Peru	USA	Pakistan	CIS	Ghana	UK	Japan	France
Life expectancy	3	5	2	4	2	4	5	5
Illiteracy (unable to read and write)	3	2	4	1	4	2	2	2
TV ownership	2	5	2	4	1	4	5	4
Access to telephones	2	5	1	2	1	4	4	4
Car ownership	2	5	1	2	1	3	3	4
Railway density	2	4	3	2	1	5	4	5
% of people aged under 15 years	4	2	4	2	4	1	2	2
Income per person (average)	3	5	1	4	1	4	5	5

Development data

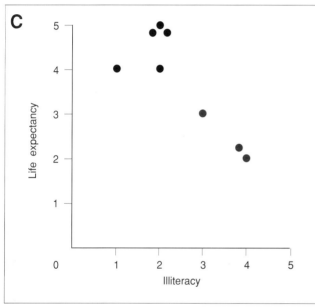

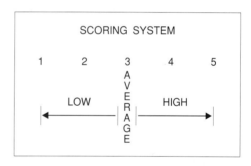

A scattergraph

4 Now look at your completed table.
- Write a few sentences to compare Peru with the control. Say how far Peru seems to show a constant pattern of characteristics of development.
- Explain why you have chosen your control option. Why do you think it provides the best comparison?

5 Study the scattergraph **C**. Work out how it has been made.
- Why do you think it is called a scattergraph?
- How well does it show a difference between North and South World countries? Explain your answer.

EXTENSION ACTIVITIES

7 Use other data from **B** to make a series of scattergraphs.
- For each scattergraph provide a comment to say:
  - How much the North and South World countries seem to be separated.
  - If the characteristic used is a good one to identify South World countries, and why.

8 Think about this hypothesis:
There is a real and significant gap between development levels in the North and South Worlds.
- How much do you now agree or disagree with this hypothesis? Explain your answer.

8.1 COMPARING THREE COUNTRIES

Targets

* To compare the locations and sizes of three major North Worlds - Japan, the USA and the CIS (Commonwealth of Independent States).
* To examine some similarities and differences in their trade and **employment structures**.
* To use and make **proportional shape** and pie chart diagrams.

Japan, the United States of America (USA) and the Commonwealth of Independent States (CIS) are three of the world's most powerful regions.

The information in this unit can be used to compare their locations and sizes.

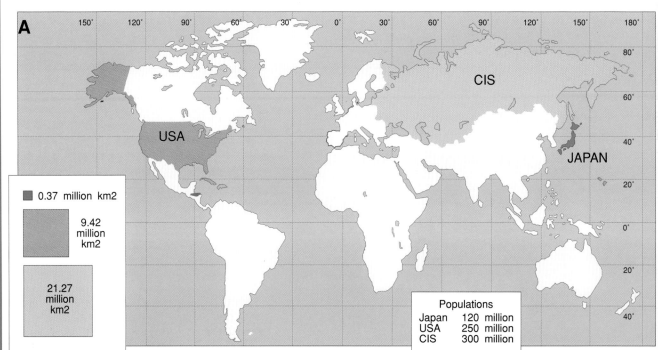

Populations
Japan   120 million
USA   250 million
CIS   300 million

Japan, the USA and CIS - locations and sizes

CORE ACTIVITIES

1 Look carefully at **A**.
- Collect data from it to help complete a copy of table **B**.
- Use your completed table to write the first two paragraphs of an essay entitled 'A Comparison of Japan, the USA and the CIS'. (*HINT*: Paragraph 1 will introduce the countries by saying where they are located and paragraph 2 will compare their area and population sizes.)

2 Study the proportional squares in **A**.
- Make proportional squares to compare the population sizes of the three countries. (*HINT*: It is the area of the square that is important, NOT the length of its sides. So, to make proportional squares you need to do two calculations:
  - find the square roots of the populations
  - scale the square roots up or down to suitable sizes.)

3 Using **C**:
- Complete a copy of the trade data table.
- Then use the employment structure data to make a pie chart. (*HINT*: A circle has 360°. So every 1 per cent is 3.6°.)

4 Study your completed trade data table and pie chart carefully.
- Use the information you have about employment structures and trade to add two further paragraphs to the essay from Activity 2.
- To finish your essay, write a final paragraph to summarise briefly how similar or different the three countries seem on the basis of the data you have.

B	JAPAN	USA	CIS
LOCATION **Description**	Islands on the western rim of the Pacific Ocean, off the eastern coast of Asia.		
Latitude	c.30-c.50°N		
Longitude	c.130-c.145°E		
SIZE **Area (m km²)**	0.37		
Population (m)	120		

Source **C** includes a pie chart presenting trade data for Japan, the USA and the CIS. Employment structure data are also given by **C**.

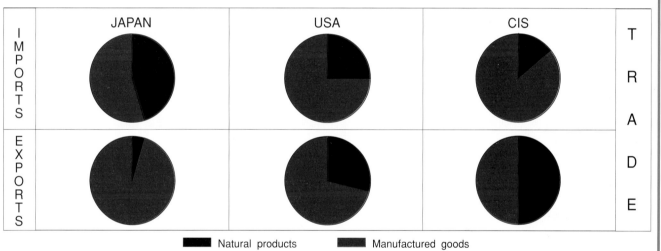

Natural products ▮   Manufactured goods ▮

	JAPAN	USA	CIS
EMPLOYMENT STRUCTURE (%)			
Primary jobs	12	2	20
Secondary	40	32	33
Tertiary/quaternary	48	66	47

	JAPAN	USA	CIS
TRADE (US dollars per person per year)			
Imports: Natural products Manufactured goods			
Exports: Natural products Manufactured goods			

Employment structure and trade

EXTENSION ACTIVITIES

5 ● Investigate other proportional shapes, apart from squares. See if you can make proportional circles, triangles or rectangles to show areas and populations.
  ● Compare the shapes you have now used. (*HINT*: Think about ease of making them as well as how well they present the data.)

Targets

* To be aware of the availability of energy resources in Japan, the USA and the CIS.
* To consider the effects of energy availability on the countries' trade in fuels.

The principal sources of energy in Japan, the USA and the CIS are shown by maps on this page.

Sea transport is an important means of moving oil around the world.

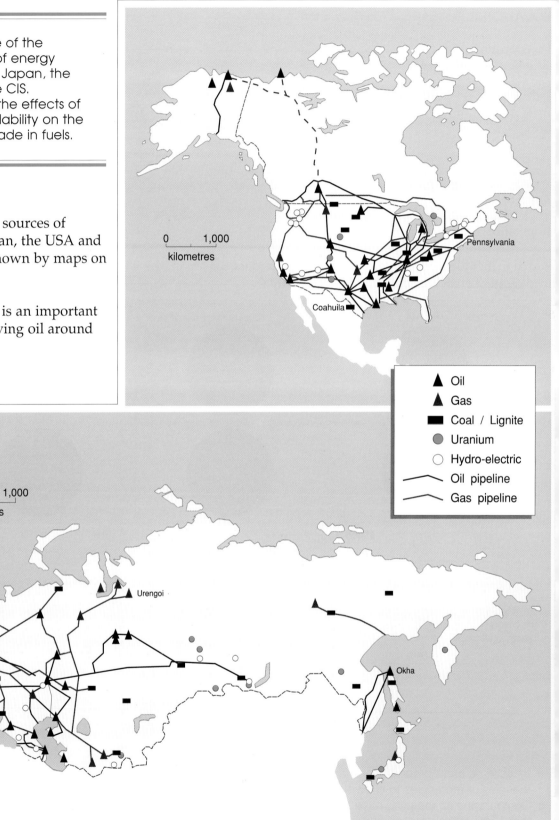

Sources of energy in the USA, CIS and Japan

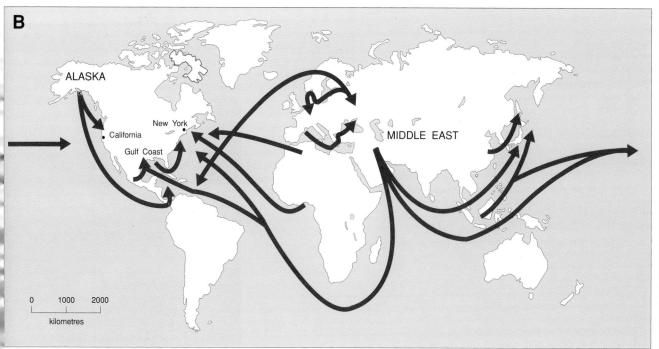

B

ALASKA

New York

California

Gulf Coast

MIDDLE EAST

0   1000   2000
kilometres

Sea transport of oil to and from the three regions

CORE ACTIVITIES

1 Using **A**:
- Make a table to compare the energy sources of the USA, CIS and Japan. (*HINT*: Use one column for each region and divide the rows between renewable and non-renewable sources of energy. Record the number of locations of each source of energy in each region. EXAMPLE: There are two coalfields shown in Japan.)
- For each of the three countries, write a description of the distribution of its energy sources. (*HINT*: You could start the USA description like this: *America's coalfields are all in the east and centre of the country. They stretch from Coahuila on the Mexican border to Pennsylvania in the north-east USA. Oilfields are ...* For the CIS it may be useful to have a map showing the names of the republics which make up the country.)

2 Look carefully at your completed table from Activity 1, as well as **A**.
- Which of the three regions will be most likely to import large amounts of oil? Why?
- Which port is at the terminal of the oil pipeline from the Okha oilfield in the eastern CIS? (*HINT*: Atlas.) Suggest a likely foreign customer for this oil.

3 Look at map **B**.
- Describe carefully exactly what this map shows about the trade in fuels of the three countries.

4 Look again at **A**.
Like all sources of information this map has limits.
- What does the map not show about:
  - the sources whose locations are marked
  - renewable sources of energy
  - the movement of oil and gas?
- Now see if you can research additional information to fill some of the gaps you have identified.

Targets

* To examine case studies of energy development in Japan, the USA and the CIS.
* To relate these case studies to the political and economic organisations of the countries.

Oil and gas are non-renewable sources of energy which are found in both the USA and the CIS. However, there are no significant local sources of oil in Japan, which relies heavily on oil imports, especially from the Middle East.

A

Oil power at Yokosuka, near Tokyo, Japan

B

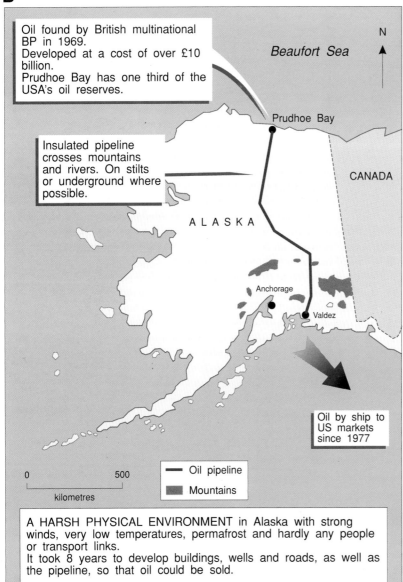

Oil found by British multinational BP in 1969.
Developed at a cost of over £10 billion.
Prudhoe Bay has one third of the USA's oil reserves.

Insulated pipeline crosses mountains and rivers. On stilts or underground where possible.

Beaufort Sea

N

Prudhoe Bay

CANADA

ALASKA

Anchorage

Valdez

Oil by ship to US markets since 1977

0   500
kilometres

— Oil pipeline
▬ Mountains

A HARSH PHYSICAL ENVIRONMENT in Alaska with strong winds, very low temperatures, permafrost and hardly any people or transport links.
It took 8 years to develop buildings, wells and roads, as well as the pipeline, so that oil could be sold.

Alaskan oil

CORE ACTIVITIES

1 You will need an outline sketch of photo **A**.
   ● Label these features:
     - flat **reclaimed land**
     - oil storage tanks
     - **oil-fired power station**
     - jetties
     - deep water channel
     - pollution
     - dock

2 Now look closely at the photograph.
   ● Write a description of the scene in the photograph, using your labels as a guide.
   ● Explain what these mean:
     - reclaimed land
     - oil-fired power station
   ● Explain why each of these factors helps make the site in photo **A** a good one for an oil-fired power station:
     - **relief**
     - **communications**
     - **market**
     - non-residential area
   ● Why does Japan need coastal oil-fired power stations like the one at Yokosuka?

C

THE SIBERIAN GAS PIPELINE

The CIS has the greatest reserves of gas in the world, and the gas field at Urengoi on the north coast of Siberia is the world's biggest. It is here that the pipeline begins. Developed in the 1980s to pipe gas nearly 5 000 km to Uzhgorod on the border with Czechoslovakia, the pipe itself was laid underground. Natural obstacles have been overcome - permafrost, river crossings, mountain ranges - as well as the internal borders between different republics within the CIS.

Much of the gas is sold in the EC, and countries like Germany, France and Britain supplied technology for the pipeline development. However, the US government felt this would make the EC too dependent on the then communist CIS for gas and tried to stop the project. After an international argument they allowed it to go ahead, though some American companies lost money.

The Siberian gas pipeline

D

	ORGANISATION	JAPAN	USA	CIS
P O L I T I C A L	SYSTEM	Democracy. Free elections. Emperor a figurehead only.	Democracy. Free elections. Elected president.	Communist until 1991. Free elections began in late 1980s/early 1990s.
	REGIONAL DIVISIONS	Prefectures. Powerful national government in Tokyo.	States. Each has own government. Federal government in Washington.	Union of separate national republics. Until late 1980s central government dominated, then balance began to change.
E C O N O M I C	SYSTEM	Capitalist. Free enterprise.	Capitalist. Free enterprise.	Communist since 1917, adopting free enterprise since late 1980s.
	ENTERPRISES	Many large multinational corporations.	Many large multinationals.	No multinationals. Traditionally under state control, but changing.

Political and economic organisation in the 3 countries

3 Look at **B** and read the information carefully.
- Use **B** to write an article called 'The Development of Oil in Alaska', in your own words.

4 Read **C** about the Siberian gas pipeline.
- Make a map to show the route of this pipeline.
- How did political and economic factors affect its development? (*HINT*: Refer to **D**.)

EXTENSION ACTIVITY

5 Study **D**.
- In what ways do you think politics and economics affected the development of oil in Alaska and the construction of the Yokosuka oil-fired power station?

Targets

* To compare patterns of industrial location in Japan, the USA and the CIS using the example of steel making.
* To understand the factors affecting the location of steel industries in the three countries.
* To be able to classify industries as light or heavy.

Steel making is a heavy industry which uses large quantities of raw materials. Japan lacks its own reserves of the essential raw materials of **coking coal** and **iron ore**. As a result Japan's steel industry has to import them and is located on the coast.

Heavy industry in Japan

Steel locations in the USA are shown in map **C**, and information about the CIS pattern is given in **D**.

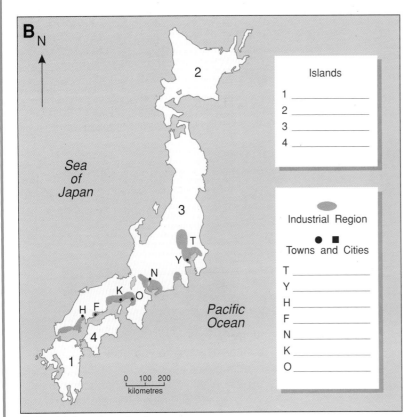

Industrial regions in Japan

CORE ACTIVITIES

1 You will need an outline sketch of photo **A**.
  ● On it locate and label the steelworks.
  ● Add these captions to your sketch, using arrows:
    - Reclaimed land provides plentiful flat space for the works.
    - A coastal location allows easy import of raw materials (coking coal and iron ore).
    - Deep water channels allow bulk carrier ships easy access.

2 Look at map **B**.
  ● Complete the key. (*HINT*: Refer to an atlas.)
  ● Describe the distribution of the industrial regions.
  ● Make a list of FOUR factors which help explain the pattern.

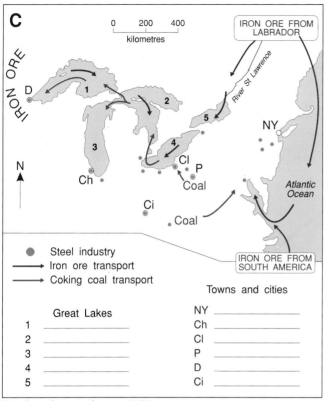

C

IRON ORE FROM LABRADOR

0   200   400
kilometres

IRON ORE

River St Lawrence

N

NY

Atlantic Ocean

Cl
P
Coal

Ch

Ci

Coal

IRON ORE FROM SOUTH AMERICA

- ● Steel industry
- → Iron ore transport
- → Coking coal transport

Towns and cities

Great Lakes

Great Lakes		Towns and cities	
1	_____	NY	_____
2	_____	Ch	_____
3	_____	Cl	_____
4	_____	P	_____
5	_____	D	_____
		Ci	_____

Steel in the north-east USA

---

3 Use your atlas to help complete map **C**'s key.
- ● Now write a description of the location of steel works in the north-east USA.
- ● How is it similar to and how is it different from the Japanese pattern?

4 Read **D**.
- ● How far do you agree or disagree with this statement?
  - - The location of steelworks is affected by the same factors and shows the same patterns the world over.
- ● Explain the reasons for your answer. (*HINT*: How many countries is this unit about?)

5 Make a table about steel industry location as follows:

Factors affecting location	Explanation
1. Flat land	Easier to build and run a large factory

- ● Now complete it from the information on these pages. The first row has been done for you, as an example.

D **DISTRIBUTION**	Five major industrial regions produce most of the steel in the CIS. They are Ukraine, the Ural zone around the towns of Magnitogorsk and Nizhniy Tagil, the Kuzbass region around Novokuznetsk, the Centre Region around Moscow, Gorki and Tula and the St Petersburg area.
RAW MATERIALS	Coking coal and iron ore have been important location factors in the CIS (as in Japan and the USA). Most iron ore is mined east of the Urals - two Siberian exceptions are Petrovsk and Kochura.
MARKETS	The biggest steel user is the engineering industry, which is widely distributed over the CIS so that communications are vital. This is equally true for the Pittsburgh works in the USA.
POLITICAL AND ECONOMIC ORGANISATION	Until recently the market has been less important in the CIS than in the capitalist USA and Japan. Steel locations were planned by the communist government to match raw material locations rather than being decided upon by companies to make profits.

Steel in the CIS

EXTENSION ACTIVITIES

6 ● Write down as many manufacturing industries as you can - at least ten. EXAMPLES: steel, cars, food processing, electronics.
- ● Now classify them into light and heavy industries.

7 Research and map the steel industry locations of two other countries.
- ● Do they seem similar to or different from countries in this unit? In what ways?
- ● Explain the patterns using the factors from Activity 5.

Targets

* To find out about patterns of industrial development in Japan, the USA and the CIS.
* To examine how these patterns are affected by the political and economic organisation of the three countries.

Industrial patterns are changing in USA and the CIS.

The headlines in **C** highlight the growing importance of **consumer goods** in industrial development. The Fact Box gives facts about consumer industries and their location.

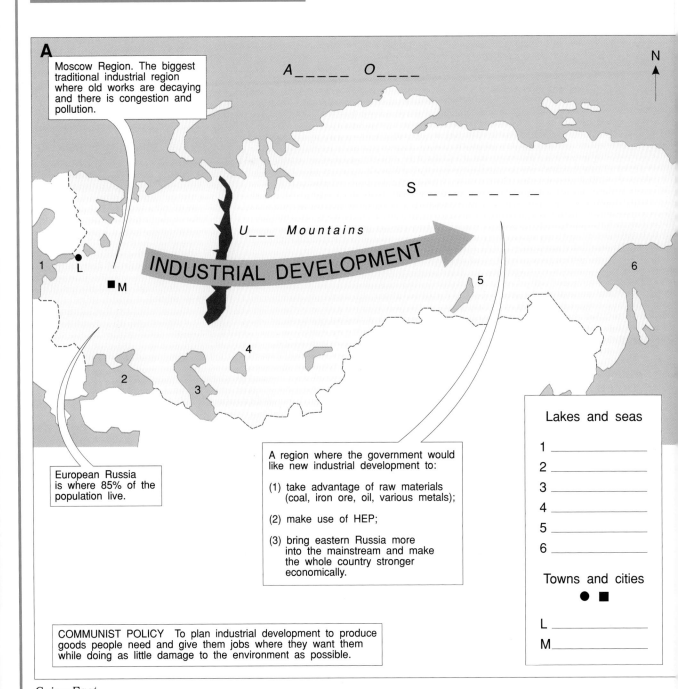

A

Moscow Region. The biggest traditional industrial region where old works are decaying and there is congestion and pollution.

A_____ O____

N

S _ _ _ _ _ _

U___ Mountains

INDUSTRIAL DEVELOPMENT

1 L

■ M

2

3

4

5

6

European Russia is where 85% of the population live.

A region where the government would like new industrial development to:

(1) take advantage of raw materials (coal, iron ore, oil, various metals);

(2) make use of HEP;

(3) bring eastern Russia more into the mainstream and make the whole country stronger economically.

Lakes and seas

1 _____
2 _____
3 _____
4 _____
5 _____
6 _____

Towns and cities
● ■

L _____
M_____

COMMUNIST POLICY   To plan industrial development to produce goods people need and give them jobs where they want them while doing as little damage to the environment as possible.

Going East

B

HEADING SOUTH

The USA has seen a modern movement of industry southwards from the old heavy industrial heartland of the north-east to the 'Sun Belt' of its southern states.

States such as Georgia, Texas, Colorado and California make up a belt stretching across America from the Pacific coast to the Appalachian Mountains where sunnier climates have attracted modern consumer and high-tech industries.

These industries are footloose - they can locate where there are good links to a market. This is because they are light industries which do not depend on bulky raw materials.

'If,' as one industrialist told our reporter, 'you can be in the sun, in a green environment with plenty of space to expand and build up-to-date facilities, and have excellent air and road links to carry components and finished goods, why be in the smoky, polluted, old, decaying North? You make money in the South and that's what we're in business for.'

Heading South

C

Consumer boom in CIS?

Japan's new industries: where to go?

FACT BOX

- In the late 1980s and early 1990s the CIS adopted a system which allowed greater free enterprise and there was a growing demand for market-led consumer industries. Where would they locate?
- High-tech footloose industries exist in Japan - an overcrowded and mountainous country. Would industry have far to move? Could there be a Japanese Sun Belt?

Headlines

CORE ACTIVITIES

1 Look at **A**. Some labels are missing.
- Use an atlas to complete the labels and the key.
- Describe the pattern of industrial development which map **A** shows.
- Make a list of reasons for this pattern.

2 Study the information in **B**.
- Design and make a map to show this information. (*HINT*: Use map **A** for clues.)

3 Look back to **D** in Unit 8.3.
- State the basic differences in political and economic organisation between the CIS and the USA.
- Explain how these differences have affected the changes shown in **A** and **B**.

4 Read the newspaper headlines in **C**.
- For each headline, write the article which may have appeared beneath. (*HINT*: Use the Fact Box for ideas.)

EXTENSION ACTIVITY

5 Patterns of industrial location are developing in Britain and the rest of the EC too.
- Collect information to help make a map for Britain or for the EC which is the equivalent of map **A**.

9.1 ONE SMALL WORLD

Targets

* To realise that our lives are linked with people and places all over the world - that the world's people depend on each other.
* To be aware that there are contrasts in development between different parts of the world.
* To read and make choropleth maps.

Our local surroundings may show many sorts of links with people and places from around the world, as may our lives themselves. In **B** Jamie and Karen discuss how their lives are linked to the world as a whole. We live in an **interdependent** world of development.

Although different parts of the world are closely linked, there are contrasts in development. Table **C** and map **D** give data about different aspects of development in a range of world countries. We live in an unequal world of development.

Local-world links

CORE ACTIVITIES

1 Look carefully at **A**.
  * Complete this table about the links which **A** shows:

Food	Shops sell tropical fruit like mangos
Travel	People can buy holidays all over the world
Clothes	
Industry	
Environment	

2 Read Jamie and Karen's discussion.
  * On an outline world map:
    - shade all the countries that they mention
    - draw linking arrows to connect these countries to the UK
    - use labels to describe each link briefly

3 Discuss in a small group how your lives are linked with the world. (*HINT*: Think carefully about links which are different from Jamie and Karen's.)
  * Repeat Activity 2, this time to show how your life is linked with the world.

Jamie, Karen and the world

C

Country	Life Expectancy (years)	Hospital Beds (people per bed)	Clean Water (% people with access)	Average annual income ($ per person)
UK	66-75	under 200	over 75	
Brazil	56-65	200-500	50-75	
China	66-75	200-500	50-75	
Zimbabwe	56-75	200-500	25-50	
India	56-65	over 1000	50-75	
Burkina Faso	under 45	over 1000	under 25	
Japan	over 75	under 200	over 75	
Malaysia	66-75	200-500	over 75	
Peru	56-65	500-1000	25-50	
Spain	over 75	under 200	over 75	
USA	over 75	under 200	over 75	
Egypt	56-65	200-500	over 75	
Romania	66-75	under 200	50-75	
Jamaica	66-75	200-500	50-75	
Indonesia	under 45	over 1000	under 25	

Data table showing aspects of development

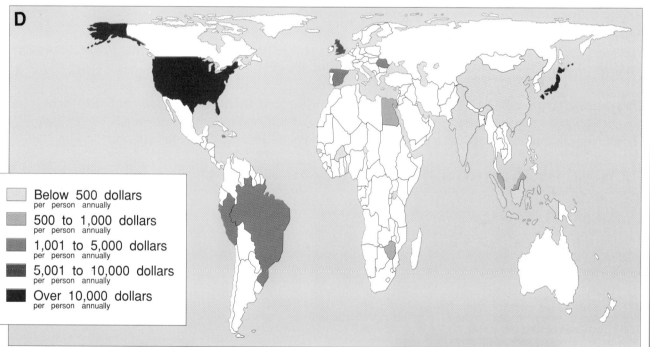

Below 500 dollars per person annually

500 to 1,000 dollars per person annually

1,001 to 5,000 dollars per person annually

5,001 to 10,000 dollars per person annually

Over 10,000 dollars per person annually

Choropleth map of average incomes

4 Look at **C** and **D**. Make sure you understand them.
- Complete table **C** by using choropleth map **D**, and then make your own choropleth maps using the rest of table **C**'s data.
- On each of the maps you have made, draw a line to divide the less well-off from the better-off countries.
- Compare your lines with the North-South World dividing line shown by map **B** in Unit 3.1. Write down how they are the same and how they are different.

EXTENSION ACTIVITIES

5 For a shopping area near you.
- Make a chart or a sketch map to show local-world links.

6 Karen has seen a poster about Africa with this message:
Don't ask how many hospitals we are building, ask how many water pumps we're putting in.
- What do you think this poster is trying to say about development?

9.2 TRADING WORLD

Targets

* To know that the world is linked by trade, but that there is an imbalance between the North and South World.
* To understand that this imbalance is largely a result of **colonialism**.
* To be aware of the role of multinational companies in world trade.
* To think how individual people can help make trade fairer.

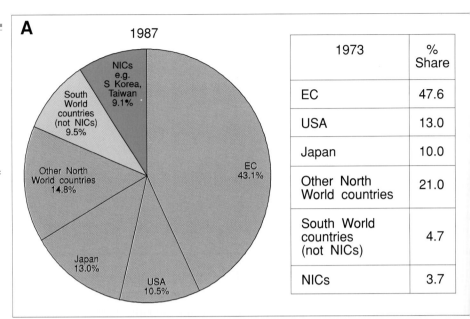

1973	% Share
EC	47.6
USA	13.0
Japan	10.0
Other North World countries	21.0
South World countries (not NICs)	4.7
NICs	3.7

Pie chart (1987): EC 43.1%, USA 10.5%, Japan 13.0%, Other North World countries 14.8%, South World countries (not NICs) 9.5%, NICs e.g. S Korea, Taiwan 9.1%

World trade in manufactured goods (NIC = Newly Industrialised Countries)

The world's countries export and import. In other words they trade. They do this to obtain goods and services for their people and to make money to develop.

Imports and exports between North and South World countries differ. **A** shows how different groups of countries share the trade in **manufactured goods**, as well as how this pattern has been changing. Some people think it is an unfair pattern, which is largely the result of **colonialism**.

An issue in world trade, and in development, is the role played by multinational companies.

World trade involves us, and so does its fairness, as Kerry explains in **D**.

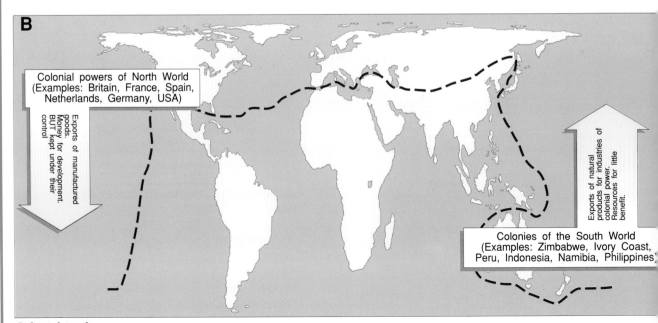

B

Colonial powers of North World (Examples: Britain, France, Spain, Netherlands, Germany, USA)

Exports of manufactured goods. Money for development. BUT kept under their control

Exports of natural products for industries of colonial power. Resources for little benefit.

Colonies of the South World (Examples: Zimbabwe, Ivory Coast, Peru, Indonesia, Namibia, Philippines)

Colonial trade

The multinational debate

CORE ACTIVITIES

1 Read these pages carefully.
- State two reasons why countries trade.

2 Using **A**:
- Copy and complete this paragraph:
  The biggest share of world trade in manufactured goods is held by the countries of the _____ at _____ per cent. Altogether, the share of the North World countries adds up to _____ per cent. Apart from Newly Industrialised Countries like _____ _____ and _____, South World countries have only a _____ per cent share.
- Use the data in the table in **A** to make another pie chart.
- Use the two pie charts to write three sentences about changes in world trade.
- Why do you think the US share of world trade in manufactured goods seems so small?

3 Now look at **B**.
- Use the diagram to write your own explanation of how colonialism has shaped today's world trade.

4 Read the TV discussion in **C**.
- Write a sentence to explain what we mean by multinational companies.
- Make a scales diagram to show the advantages and disadvantages of multinational companies for development, and which side of the argument (if any) you come down on.

5 Think about what Kerry says in **D**.
- Make a poster to help publicise her ideas.
- What is your opinion of what Kerry says?

Kerry says . . .

EXTENSION ACTIVITY

6 Find out more about multinational companies.
- Who are they? Where are they based? What do they make that you use?
  (*HINT*: Look back to Module 6, use other books and look for their adverts in magazines, newspapers and on television.)

9.3 POPULATION DISTRIBUTION

Targets

* To know that people are not evenly spread over the world.
* To understand reasons why some regions are only sparsely settled.
* To understand how the populations of countries change in size.
* To be aware that migration can affect the make-up, as well as the size, of populations.

In the 60 years from 1930 to 1990, the population of the world more than doubled, from 2 000 million people to over 5 000 million people. Where do these people live?

A is a map of world population distribution. It shows that **population density** is not even. There are regions of the world where the population density is very low.

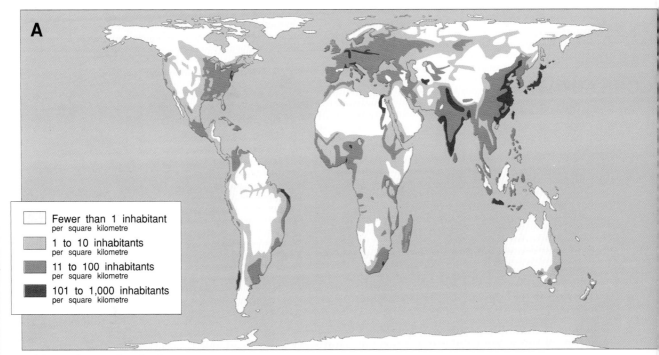

A

Fewer than 1 inhabitant
per square kilometre

1 to 10 inhabitants
per square kilometre

11 to 100 inhabitants
per square kilometre

101 to 1,000 inhabitants
per square kilometre

World population distribution

CORE ACTIVITIES

1 Look at map **A**.
  * For each of the world's continents, describe the distribution of regions of sparse population. EXAMPLE: In North America the main areas of low population density are in the far north and the western half of the USA, away from the coast.
  (*HINT*: Remember Antarctica!)

2 On an outline map of Australia:
  * Make your own map of population distribution.
  * Locate these cities: Sydney, Melbourne, Brisbane, Adelaide, Perth.   (*HINT*: Use your atlas.)
  * Use the information given in **B** to label your map with factors explaining why parts of Australia are sparsely populated.
  * Use your atlas to mark on your map the settlements named in **B** and add a caption to explain why these settlements have developed.

B **Why are parts of Australia sparsely populated?**	**Why are some settlements found there anyway?**
CLIMATE Much of interior Australia has a hot, dry climate. The north and north-west coasts have a hot, wet monsoon climate.	Mining of minerals, including gold, bauxite and iron ore. *Examples: Kalgoorlie, Mt Tom Price, Yampi Sound.*
ACCESSIBILITY Australia has been populated largely by migrants, who preferred to settle near the ports where they arrived and where jobs were to be found.	Transport links. *Examples: Alice Springs - railhead and airport, Darwin - northern port.* Farming: scattered cattle stations (ranches).

Why are parts of Australia sparsely populated?

3 **C** shows the population growth rates for selected countries.
- Using data from **C**, make a choropleth map of population growth rates in selected countries.
- Study your map and think about this hypothesis: *Population growth rates are much greater in South World countries than in the North World.*
- Do you agree, disagree or partly agree? Why? (*HINT*: Australia is usually classed as a North World country.)

4 Read the following sentences.
- Complete each one by choosing words from the list at the end:
  Population _____ is the pattern of where people live.
  A place where people live is called a _____
  Population _____ is how many people live in each square kilometre.
  A sparsely settled region has a _____ population density.

settlement	*high*	*low*
density	*distribution*	*migration*

5 Read **D**.
- Explain how migration can affect the ethnic, cultural and religious composition of a country's population, using Australia as your example.

The population is growing more quickly in some countries than in others, as table **C** shows. Migration changes the size of national populations. It also affects population make-up.

C Country	**POPULATION GROWTH RATE** (% per year)
Australia	1.4
Brazil	2.2
China	1.2
India	2.1
Indonesia	2.1
Nigeria	3.4
Pakistan	3.1
CIS	0.9
United Kingdom	0.2
United States	1.0

Population growth

D

Migration and Australians

EXTENSION ACTIVITIES

6 Find out about migrations in other parts of the world.
- Record their effects on the ethnic, religious and cultural make-up of their populations.

Targets

* To be aware of who gives **aid** and who receives it.
* To consider the issue of whether aid helps development.

Below are examples of **aid** adverts. Adverts like these often appear in our newspapers.

People have different views about the usefulness of aid in development.

A

NOW Muslim Aid in RAMADAN

IS THE TIME FOR DUTY

Comfortable in our armchairs, it is all too easy to forget reality in front of TV. Disasters, natural and man-made, are all-too-frequent viewing. But these starving, bereaved, shocked and grieving people are not actors. There is no happy ending for them. Their suffering goes on; we look on …

While you have a meal tonight, **20 million people are STARVING IN AFRICA alone.** The list seems endless.
Sudan, Ethiopia, Somalia, Mozambique, Bangladesh, Afghanistan, Palestine, Lebanon **and now THE GULF.**

The price of one week's bombs could feed Africa for a year. But that is too much to hope for. Now it is Ramadan. And now it is our duty to help them.

"And in their wealth the needy and the deprived have a right."
Qur'an 51:19

Please rush your Zakah, Sadaqah, and donations to:
Muslim Aid
P.O. Box 3, London N7 8LR
Tel: 071-609 4425
Reg. Charity No: 295224.

B

HELP US BUILD FOR HER FUTURE

If you care about the welfare of the elderly, this is your chance to do something positive.

Servite Houses Ltd and Help The Aged are currently building 100 new homes for the elderly, in the heart of London.

So far we have achieved half of our target figure of £2m, which leaves a desperately needed £1,000,000 to raise.

Once completed these homes will be of invaluable benefit to the elderly in need, the frail elderly and the confused elderly.

But we need *your* help.

If you are willing to respond, all donations will be gratefully received. Please send cheque or postal orders payable to Servite Houses Ltd to:

Joan Bartlett, O.B.E., Hon. Director,
Servite Houses Battersea Appeal,
125 Old Brompton Road,
London SW7 3RP.

Views about aid

CORE ACTIVITIES

1 Look at **A** and **B**.
  - Name the two charities which placed the adverts.
  - Make a 2-column table showing the places they say they have helped and what they have done.

2 Imagine receiving a leaflet from a charity like those in **A** and **B**.
  - What would you do with it? Why?

3 Put yourself in the place of one of the people pictured in adverts **A** and **B**. The photographer asks you how you feel about your photo being used in a charity aid advert.
  - Write down your reply.

4 Look at **C**.
  - Where does most aid come from?
  - What do people mean by 'boomerang' aid?
  - Do you think 'boomerang aid' is a good or bad thing? Why?
  - 'Aid is help for people hit by natural disasters like earthquakes or hurricanes.' Do you agree? Explain your answer.
  - Describe an example of useful aid which is not expensive.

5 Make a collection of aid adverts.
  - Map the places they mention and describe the distribution of the places they want to help.

6 Find out other people's responses to the leaflet in Activity 2.
  - Graph the results.

7 'I've done my bit for the South. I ran in a sponsored race.'
  - Think about whether the person who said this has 'done her bit'. What else can people do to help? (*HINT*: Try to think of ways apart from giving money.)

9.5 REAL DEVELOPMENT AND ME

Targets

* To think about the directions that developments should take.
* To consider what actions we can each take to influence development.

Developments are real changes - they affect people and the environment. 'Real developments' improve the quality of life for people and also fit in with the environment.

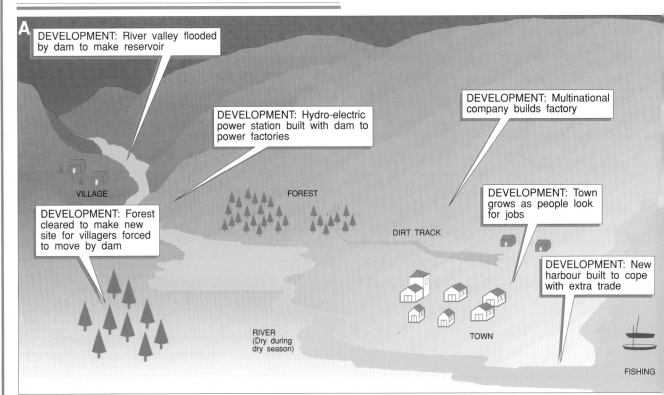

A

DEVELOPMENT: River valley flooded by dam to make reservoir

DEVELOPMENT: Hydro-electric power station built with dam to power factories

DEVELOPMENT: Multinational company builds factory

DEVELOPMENT: Forest cleared to make new site for villagers forced to move by dam

DEVELOPMENT: Town grows as people look for jobs

DEVELOPMENT: New harbour built to cope with extra trade

VILLAGE

FOREST

DIRT TRACK

RIVER (Dry during dry season)

TOWN

FISHING

Real development?

CORE ACTIVITIES

1 Look at **A**.
- Make a list of four developments which have taken place.
- Write down how each of the developments in your list has affected:
  - the local people
  - the environment
  (*HINT*: Try to think of good, as well as bad, effects.)

2 Read the following statement:
Building the reservoir is not real development.
- Do you think this is true? Explain your reasons.

3 Imagine that photo **B** is the view from your bedroom window.
- On an outline sketch of photo **B**, label the features which you think makes your view look attractive.

4 A neighbour has told you that there is a plan to build 400 houses on the hill you overlook.
- How do you feel about this planned development? (*HINT*: Remember that people need homes.)
- Make a labelled sketch to show how it will affect the environment.

5 Your neighbour says there's nothing that anybody can do about this development.
- What can you do:
  - if you oppose the development?
  - if you agree with the development?

Below are some views about development what it means and how we can each act to influence development, to make sure it is real development.

'Not in my backyard!'

C

BUYING CRAFTS AND THINGS LIKE TEA FROM A THIRD WORLD TRADE SHOP HELPS PEOPLE IN THE SOUTH MAKE A LIVING.

READING AND FINDING OUT ABOUT THE SOUTH WORLD HELPS PEOPLE OF THE WORLD TO UNDERSTAND EACH OTHER BETTER.

USING RECYCLED PAPER HELPS TO STOP TOO MANY TREES FROM BEING CUT DOWN AND THE GREENHOUSE EFFECT FROM GETTING TOO BAD AND HARMING EVERYBODY.

CHOOSING TO BUY PRODUCTS WHICH ARE ENVIRONNENTALLY FRIENDLY REDUCES DAMAGE TO OUR ENVIRONMENT.

RAISING MONEY FOR AID CHARITIES HELPS POOR PEOPLE EVERYWHERE – IN THE NORTH AND THE SOUTH WORLD

WRITING LETTERS TO PEOPLE IN POWER SHOWS OUR CONCERN OVER DEVELOPMENT ISSUES.

JOINING GROUPS WHICH CAMPAIGN FOR REAL DEVELOPMENT HELPS TO RAISE PEOPLES' AWARENESS ABOUT WORLD INEQUALITIES.

6 Read the action ideas in **C**.
  ● Use them to complete this table:

Global Thought	Local Action
Help South World people make their own living	
	Use recycled paper

7 Think about the entries in your table.
  ● Which do you think are the most useful and the least useful ways to influence development?

EXTENSION ACTIVITY

8 Look back through this book at some case study developments.
  ● For each:
    - write down what the development is
    - decide whether or not you think it is real development, and why
    - think about what effects it has had on the environment and on people
    - consider how local action may have influenced the development.

GLOSSARY

A

Agribusiness	the big business of growing and marketing food
Agriculture	farming
Aid	help for countries and people
Alternative energy	power from a different source, such as sugar cane used to fuel cars
Appropriate technology	suitable ways of doing things

B

Birth rate	the number of babies born per thousand people in a year

C

Calorie	a unit to measure the energy people get from food
Capital	money used to invest, to develop
Capital city	the main city of a country where a government is based
Cassava	a tropical root crop whose flour can be used to make bread
Census	a survey to count people and collect other population data
Central Business District (CBD)	the city centre
Choropleth map	a map using shaded areas to present data
Climate graph	a diagram made up of a bar graph to show rainfall and a line graph to show temperature
Coking coal	good quality coal which can be made into coke
Colonialism	the system of powerful countries taking control of and running other countries.
Colonists	the people who practise colonialism
Colonies	the countries taken over by the powerful
Communications	links between places
Components	parts used in industry to assemble goods
Congestion	traffic becoming so busy that it slows down or stops
Consumer goods	goods made to sell to the public
Conventional energy source	a usual form of power, such as oil for petrol to fuel a car
Costs	the opposite to the benefits of developments - to the environment and people as well as in money

D

Death rate	the number of people who die, out of every thousand, each year
Developer	a person who makes changes, usually involving building
Developing cities	changing cities
Developments	changes intended to help people
Distribution	spread

E

Earth's crust	the thin shell of solid rock which surrounds the Earth
EC	European Community - a group of European countries which work closely together
Economic costs	costs in money
Emigration	moving away from a place to live somewhere else
Employment structure	the proportions of jobs in the primary, secondary and tertiary/quaternary sectors
Energy	power for warmth, cooking and to drive machines, for example
Entrepot	a port with the function of unloading cargo from one type of transport and reloading it on to another
Environment	our total surroundings
Environmental groups	groups which try to protect our surroundings from harmful development
Exports	goods and services sold abroad

F	Factors	reasons which add together to explain something
	Fertilisers	nutrients added to the soil to improve it
	Functions	jobs which places have, such as being a port
G	Greenfield site	a piece of land which has not been built on before
	Green Revolution	a great increase in food production because of development
	Gross national product (GNP)	the total value of a country's production in a year
H	Heavy industry	an industry using bulky raw materials to make heavy goods
	Hectare	an area of 10 000 m^2
	Hydro-electric power (HEP)	electricity generated using the power of fast-flowing water
	Hypothesis	a statement which can be tested to see if it is true
I	Immigration	moving into a country to live there
	Imports	goods and services bought in from abroad
	Industrial	anything to do with industry and especially with factories
	Inequality	unfairness
	Infant mortality	the number of babies who die without growing beyond infancy
	Interdependent	relying on each other
	Internal migration	moving within a country
	Iron ore	the natural and impure form of iron in the Earth's crust
	Irrigation	bringing water to a place to water the land
L	Labour supply	the availability of people as a workforce
	Landlocked	having no coasts
	Land reform	changing how land is owned
	Latitude	how far a place is north or south of the equator, measured in degrees
	Location	where a place is
	Longitude	how far east or west a place is, measured in degrees
M	Maize	a cereal crop often called corn or sweetcorn
	Manufactured goods	products made by industry from raw materials or components
	Market	where goods are sold, e.g. a place, a company, an industry
	Mechanisation	changing over to using machines
	Migrants	people who migrate
	Migration	moving between places to live
	Multinational companies	firms with businesses in more than one country
N	Natural increase	the growth in population which is the difference between the birth rate and the death rate
	Non-renewable energy	power which, once used, cannot be replaced
	Nuclear power	electricity from atomic reactions
O	Oil-fired power station	a building which makes electricity by burning oil to boil water to make steam and drive turbines
P	Pesticide	a chemical to kill pests
	Pie chart	a diagram made of a circle cut into sectors to show shares
	Plantation	a large farm where cash crops are grown
	Political map	an atlas map showing countries and their boundaries
	Population	the people of a place

Population density	the number of people per km²
Primary energy source	power which comes directly from the environment, e.g. coal, natural gas
Processed food	food which has been changed between being produced by the farmer and being bought by the consumer
Proportional shapes	diagrams where the area of a shape shows size
Push and pull reasons	why people leave one place and move to another place

Q Quality of life   how good life is for people, measured in different ways, e.g. in wealth or health or happiness

R
Reclaimed land	land which is made useful by people, e.g. by draining a shallow sea
Redevelopment	to change a place again
Refining oil	splitting crude oil into usable fractions, e.g. petrol
Relief	the shape of the land
Renewable energy	power which can be replaced, e.g. solar power
Residential area	a zone in a city which is mostly housing
Resources	things people take from our physical environment because they are useful
Rural-urban migration	moving from the countryside to the town to live

S
Scales diagram	a diagram to show the balance of views about a development (see Unit 1.3)
Scattergraph	a graph which has two axes and presents data as a scatter of points, to see if there are links between two data sets
Secondary energy source	power made from a primary energy source, e.g. electricity generated from coal
Self-help	people developing places for themselves
Self-sufficient	not relying on outside aid
Shanty	a part of a city with poor housing, often made by the people themselves
Soil erosion	wearing away of the soil
Solar power	energy from the rays of the sun
Sorghum	a food crop, often grown in the tropics
South, South World	the set of countries of the world which are poorer than the richer North
Surface run-off	rainwater which runs away over the ground

T
Terrace	small piece of land made flat by people, often for farming
Thermal electricity	electricity generated from heating a primary energy source like coal to make steam to drive turbines and generate electricity
Transport network	a system of links between places, e.g. roads, railways
Trend	the general direction of change

W
Water power	energy generated from running water
Wind power	energy generated by the force of the wind